"Government is the great fiction, through which everybody endeavours to live at the expense of everybody else."

— Frederic Bastiat (1801-1850)
ESSAYS ON POLITICAL ECONOMY, 1872

About the Uncle Eric Series

The Uncle Eric series of books is written by Richard J. Maybury for young and old alike. Using the epistolary style of writing (using letters to tell a story), Mr. Maybury plays the part of an economist writing a series of letters to his niece or nephew. Using stories and examples, he gives interesting and clear explanations of topics that are generally thought to be too difficult for anyone but experts.

Mr. Maybury warns, "beware of anyone who tells you a topic is above you or better left to experts. Many people are twice as smart as they think they are, but they've been intimidated into believing some topics are above them. You can understand almost anything if it is explained well."

The series is called UNCLE ERIC'S MODEL OF HOW THE WORLD WORKS. In the series, Mr. Maybury writes from the political, legal and economic viewpoint of America's Founders. The books can be read in any order, and have been written to stand alone. To get the most from each one, however, Mr. Maybury suggests the following order of reading:

Uncle Eric's Model
of How the World Works

Uncle Eric Talks About Personal, Career, and Financial Security

Whatever Happened to Penny Candy?

Whatever Happened to Justice?

Are You Liberal? Conservative? or Confused?

Ancient Rome: How It Affects You Today

Evaluating Books: What Would Thomas Jefferson Think About This?

The Money Mystery

The Clipper Ship Strategy

The Thousand Year War in the Mideast

World War I: The Rest of the Story and How It Affects You Today

World War II: The Rest of the Story and How It Affects You Today

(Study guides and/or tests are available or forthcoming for above titles.)

An Uncle Eric Book

The Clipper Ship Strategy

FOR SUCCESS IN YOUR CAREER,
BUSINESS, AND INVESTMENTS

Revised Edition

Second sequel to
WHATEVER HAPPENED TO PENNY CANDY?

by Richard J. Maybury
(Uncle Eric)

published by
Bluestocking Press
www.BluestockingPress.com

Cover illustration by Bob O'Hara, Georgetown, CA
Cover design by Brian C. Williams, El Dorado, CA
Edited by Jane A. Williams

Library of Congress Cataloging-in-Publication Data

Maybury, Rick.
    The clipper ship strategy : for success in your career, business, and investments / by Richard J. Maybury.-- Rev. ed.
        p. cm. -- (An Uncle Eric book)
Second sequel to: Whatever happened to Penny Candy?
Includes bibliographical references (p.   ) and index.
    ISBN-13: 978-0-942617-37-5 (alk. paper)
    ISBN-10:   0-942617-37-1
    1. United States--Economic conditions--1981-2001. 2. Business cycles--United States. 3. Monetary policy--United States. I. Title.

    HC106.8.M34 2003
    332.024--dc22   2003014735

Published by Bluestocking Press • P.O. Box 1014
Placerville, CA 95667-1014
web site: www.BluestockingPress.com

To Doug Casey,
who never had any obligation to help me,
but he did.

Uncle Eric's Model
of How the World Works

What is a model? In his book UNCLE ERIC TALKS ABOUT PERSONAL, CAREER, AND FINANCIAL SECURITY, Richard Maybury (Uncle Eric) explains that one of the most important things you can teach children or learn yourself is:

"Models are how we think, they are how we understand how the world works. As we go through life we build these very complex pictures in our minds of how the world works, and we're constantly referring back to them — matching incoming data against our models. That's how we make sense of things.

"One of the most important uses for models is in sorting incoming information to decide if it's important or not.

"In most schools, models are never mentioned because the teachers are unaware of them. One of the most dangerous weaknesses in traditional education is that it contains no model for political history. Teachers teach what they were taught — and no one ever mentioned models to them, so they don't teach them to their students.

"For the most part, children are just loaded down with collections of facts that they are made to memorize. Without good models, children have no way to know which facts are important and which are not. Students leave school thinking history is a senseless waste of time. Then, deprived of the real lessons of history, the student is vulnerable."

The question is, which models to teach. Mr. Maybury says, "The two models that I think are crucially important for everyone to learn are economics and law."

WHATEVER HAPPENED TO PENNY CANDY? explains the economic model, which is based on Austrian economics, the most free-market of all economic models. WHATEVER HAPPENED TO JUSTICE? explains the legal model and shows the connection between rational law and economic progress. The legal model is the old British Common Law — or Natural Law. The original principles on which America was founded were those of the old British Common Law.

These two books, PENNY CANDY and JUSTICE, provide the overall model of how human civilization works, especially the world of money.

Once the model is understood, read ARE YOU LIBERAL? CONSERVATIVE? OR CONFUSED? This book explains political philosophies relative to Uncle Eric's Model — and makes a strong case for consistency to that model, no exceptions.

Next, read ANCIENT ROME: HOW IT AFFECTS YOU TODAY, which shows what happens when a society ignores Uncle Eric's Model and embraces fascism—an all too common practice these days, although the word fascism is never used.

To help you locate books and authors generally in agreement with these economic and legal models, Mr. Maybury wrote EVALUATING BOOKS: WHAT WOULD THOMAS JEFFERSON THINK ABOUT THIS? This book provides guidelines for selecting books that are consistent with the principles of America's Founders. You can apply these guidelines to books, movies, news commentators, and current events — to any spoken or written medium.

Further expanding on the economic model, THE MONEY MYSTERY explains the hidden force affecting your career, business and investments. Some economists refer to this force as velocity, others to money demand. Whichever term is used, it is one of the least understood forces affecting your life. Knowing about velocity and money demand not only gives you an understanding of history that few others have, it prepares you to understand and avoid pitfalls in your career, business, and investments. THE MONEY MYSTERY is the first sequel to WHATEVER HAPPENED TO PENNY CANDY? It provides essential background for getting the most from THE CLIPPER SHIP STRATEGY.

THE CLIPPER SHIP STRATEGY explains how government's interference in the economy affects business, careers, and investments. It's a practical nuts-and-bolts strategy for prospering in our turbulent economy. This book is the second sequel to WHATEVER HAPPENED TO PENNY CANDY? and should be read after THE MONEY MYSTERY.

THE THOUSAND YEAR WAR IN THE MIDEAST: HOW IT AFFECTS YOU TODAY explains how events on the other side of the world a thousand years ago can affect us more than events in our own hometowns today. In the last quarter of the 20th century, the Thousand Year War has been the cause of great shocks to the investment markets — the oil embargoes, the Iranian hostage crisis, the Iraq-Kuwait war, the Caucasus Wars over the Caspian Sea oil basin, and the September 11th attack — and it is likely to remain so for decades to come. Forewarned is forearmed. You must understand where this war is leading to manage your career, business, and investments.

The explosion of the battleship Maine in Havana Harbor in 1898 was the beginning of a chain reaction that eventually led to the destruction of the World Trade Center. In his two-part World War series Richard Maybury explains that an unbroken line leads directly from the Spanish-American War through World War I, World War II, the Korean and Vietnam Wars, the Iraq-Kuwait War, and the "War on Terror" that began September 11, 2001. Mr. Maybury explains the other side of the story, the side you are not likely to get anywhere else, in this two-part World War series: WORLD WAR I: THE REST OF THE STORY AND HOW IT AFFECTS YOU TODAY and WORLD WAR II: THE REST OF THE STORY AND HOW IT AFFECTS YOU TODAY.

Uncle Eric's Model of How the World Works

These books can be read in any order and have been written to stand alone. But to get the most from each one, Mr. Maybury suggests the following order of reading:

Book 1.   UNCLE ERIC TALKS ABOUT PERSONAL, CAREER, AND FINANCIAL SECURITY.
Uncle Eric's Model introduced. Models (or paradigms) are how people think; they are how we understand our world. To achieve success in our careers, investments, and every other part of our lives, we need sound models. These help us recognize and use the information that is important and bypass that which is not. In this book, Mr. Maybury introduces the model he has found most useful. These are explained in WHATEVER HAPPENED TO PENNY CANDY? WHATEVER HAPPENED TO JUSTICE? and THE CLIPPER SHIP STRATEGY.

Book 2.   WHATEVER HAPPENED TO PENNY CANDY? A FAST, CLEAR, AND FUN EXPLANATION OF THE ECONOMICS YOU NEED FOR SUCCESS IN YOUR CAREER, BUSINESS, AND INVESTMENTS.
The economic model explained. The clearest and most interesting explanation of economics around. Learn about investment cycles, velocity, business cycles, recessions, inflation, money demand, and more. Contains "Beyond

the Basics," which supplements the basic ideas in the book and is included for readers who choose to tackle more challenging concepts. Recommended by former U.S. Treasury Secretary William Simon and many others. *(Study Guide available.)*

Book 3.   WHATEVER HAPPENED TO JUSTICE?
The legal model explained. Explores America's legal heritage. Shows what is wrong with our legal system and economy, and how to fix it. Discusses the difference between higher law and man-made law, and the connection between rational law and economic prosperity. Introduces the Two Laws: 1) Do all you have agreed to do. 2) Do not encroach on other persons or their property.

Book 4.   ARE YOU LIBERAL? CONSERVATIVE? OR CONFUSED?
Political labels. What do they mean? Liberal, conservative, left, right, democrat, republican, moderate, socialist, libertarian, communist — what are their economic policies, and what plans do their promoters have for your money? Clear, concise explanations. Facts and fallacies.

Book 5.   ANCIENT ROME: HOW IT AFFECTS YOU TODAY.
This book explains what happens when a society ignores the model. Are we heading for fascism like ancient Rome? Mr. Maybury uses historical events to explain current events, including the wars in the former Soviet Empire, and the legal and economic problems of America today. With the turmoil in Russia and Russia's return to fascism, you must read this book to understand your future. History does repeat.

Book 6.   EVALUATING BOOKS: WHAT WOULD THOMAS JEFFERSON THINK ABOUT THIS?
Most books, magazines, and news stories are slanted against the principles of America's Founders. Often the writers are not aware of it, they simply write as they were taught. Learn how to identify the bias so you can make informed reading, listening, and viewing choices.

Book 7.   THE MONEY MYSTERY: THE HIDDEN FORCE AFFECTING YOUR CAREER, BUSINESS, AND INVESTMENTS. The first sequel to WHATEVER HAPPENED TO PENNY CANDY? Some economists refer to velocity, others to money demand. However it is seen, it is one of the least understood forces affecting our businesses, careers and investments — it is the financial trigger. This book discusses precautions you should take and explains why Federal Reserve officials remain so afraid of inflation. THE MONEY MYSTERY prepares you to understand and avoid pitfalls in your career, business, and investments.

Book 8.   THE CLIPPER SHIP STRATEGY: FOR SUCCESS IN YOUR CAREER, BUSINESS, AND INVESTMENTS. The second sequel to WHATEVER HAPPENED TO PENNY CANDY? Conventional wisdom says that when the government expands the money supply, the money descends on the economy in a uniform blanket. This is wrong. The money is injected into specific locations causing hot spots or "cones" such as the tech bubble of the 1990s. Mr. Maybury explains his system for tracking and profiting from these cones. Practical nuts-and-bolts strategy for prospering in our turbulent economy.

Book 9.   THE THOUSAND YEAR WAR IN THE MIDEAST: HOW IT AFFECTS YOU TODAY. Mr. Maybury shows that events on the other side of the world a thousand years ago can affect us more than events in our hometowns today. This book explains the ten-century battle the U.S. has entered against the Islamic world. It predicted the events that began unfolding on September 11, 2001. It helps you understand the thinking of the Muslims in the Mideast, and why the coming oil war will affect investment markets around the globe. In the last three decades this war has been the cause of great shocks to the economy and investment markets, including the oil embargoes, the Iranian hostage crisis, the Iraq-Kuwait war, the Caucasus Wars over the Caspian Sea oil basin, and the September 11th attack, and it is likely to remain so for decades to come. Forewarned is forearmed. To successfully manage your career, business, and investments, you must understand this war.

Book 10. WORLD WAR I: THE REST OF THE STORY AND HOW IT AFFECTS YOU TODAY, 1870 TO 1935.
The explosion of the battleship Maine in Havana Harbor in 1898 was the beginning of a chain reaction that continues today. Mr. Maybury presents an idea-based explanation of the First World War. He focuses on the ideas and events that led to World War I, events during the war, and how they led to World War II. Includes the ten deadly ideas that lead to war.

Book 11. WORLD WAR II: THE REST OF THE STORY AND HOW IT AFFECTS YOU TODAY, 1935 TO SEPTEMBER 11, 2001.
An idea-based explanation of the war. Focuses on events in the Second World War and how our misunderstanding of this war led to America's subsequent wars, including the Korean and Vietnam Wars, the Iraq-Kuwait War, and the "War on Terror" that began September 11, 2001.

Quantity Discounts Available

The Uncle Eric books are available at special quantity discounts for bulk purchases to individuals, businesses, schools, libraries, and associations, to be distributed as gifts, premiums, or as fund raisers.

For terms and discount schedule contact:

Special Sales Department
Bluestocking Press
Phone: 800-959-8586
email: CustomerService@BluestockingPress.com
web site: www.BluestockingPress.com

Specify how books are to be distributed: for classrooms, or as gifts, premiums, fund raisers — or to be resold.

Contents

Note to Reader

Throughout each Uncle Eric book, whenever a word that appears in the glossary is introduced in the text, it is displayed in a **bold typeface**.

Author's Disclosure

For reasons I do not understand, writers today are sup-posed to be objective. Few disclose the viewpoints or opin-ions they use to decide what information is important and what is not, or what shall be presented or omitted.

I do not adhere to this standard and make no pretense of being objective. I am biased in favor of liberty, free markets, and international neutrality and proud of it. So I disclose my viewpoint, which you will find explained in detail in my other books.[1]

For those who have not yet read these publications, I call my viewpoint Juris Naturalism (pronounced *jur*-es *nach*-e-re-liz-em, sometimes abbreviated JN) meaning the belief in a natural law that is higher than any government's law. Here are six quotes from America's Founders that help to describe this viewpoint:

...all men are created equal, that they are endowed by their Creator with certain unalienable rights.
— Declaration of Independence, 1776

The natural rights of the colonists are these: first, a right to life; second to liberty; third to property; together with the right to support and defend them in the best manner they can.
— Samuel Adams, 1772

---

[1] See Richard Maybury's other Uncle Eric books (see pgs. 6-11), published by Bluestocking Press, web site: www.BluestockingPress.com.

It is strangely absurd to suppose that a million of human beings collected together are not under the same moral laws which bind each of them separately.
— Thomas Jefferson, 1816

A wise and frugal government, which shall restrain men from injuring one another, which shall leave them otherwise free to regulate their own pursuits of industry and improvement, and shall not take from the mouth of labor the bread it has earned. This is the sum of good government.
— Thomas Jefferson, 1801

Not a place on earth might be so happy as America. Her situation is remote from all the wrangling world, and she has nothing to do but to trade with them.
— Thomas Paine, 1776

The great rule of conduct for us, in regard to foreign nations, is, in extending our commercial relations, to have with them as little political connection as possible.
— George Washington, 1796

George
Washington

Part 1

Sales Strategy

The Building of the Ship

Build me straight, O worthy Master!
Stanch and strong, a goodly vessel, That shall
laugh at all disaster,
And with wave and whirlwind wrestle!"

The merchant's word
Delighted the Master heard;
For his heart was in his work, and the heart
Giveth grace unto every Art.

A quiet smile played round his lips,
As the eddies and dimples of the tide
Play round the bows of ships,
That steadily at anchor ride.
And with a voice that was full of glee,
He answered, "Erelong we will launch
A vessel as goodly, and strong, and stanch,
As ever weathered a wintry sea!

— Henry Wadsworth Longfellow

Henry Wadsworth Longfellow observed the building of the clipper ship *Flying Cloud* during the Winter/Spring of 1851. He immortalized the ship and its builder, Donald McKay, in the poem "The Building of the Ship" from which the above stanzas are excerpted.

1

A Strategy for Success

Dear Chris,

Thanks for your recent letter. You are right. In previous letters about **economics**[2] I did promise to write you in depth about a system called **Business Cycle Management (BCM)**. And, yes, I do have time now to write. I'd like to begin by telling you the story of a clipper ship called the *Flying Cloud*. It's an important story because Business Cycle Management was derived from the lessons of the *Flying Cloud*.

On June 2, 1851, the sailing ship *Flying Cloud* left New York bound for San Francisco. Making the maximum possible speed for three solid months, the ship's journey was one

---

[2] When Uncle Eric refers to his previous set of letters about economics he is referring to the book WHATEVER HAPPENED TO PENNY CANDY?, by Richard J. Maybury published by Bluestocking Press, web site: www.BluestockingPress.com, and in particular to chapter nine where he promises to write future letters to Chris that will explain the system called Business Cycle Management.

of the most exciting and dangerous in history. It was a full-speed dash around Cape Horn in the dead of the Antarctic winter.

Thanks in no small part to the skills of the ship's navigator, who was the captain's wife, the *Flying Cloud* reached San Francisco in 89 days, a record not broken until 138 years later.

Why were the *Flying Cloud's* captain and crew in such a hurry to reach San Francisco?

The answer will help you understand one of the most important lessons you will ever learn. The story of the *Flying Cloud* will help you achieve success and prosperity every day for the rest of your life.

Hard to believe? Read on.

We begin the story with the fact that in bad times as well as good, someone is always earning lots of money. Even in the Great Depression, while some people were barely getting by, others got rich. How?

I first asked myself this question during the 1980 **recession**, and in the 1982 recession began research to learn exactly what these successful workers, firms, and investors were doing right.

This research led me to the story of the *Flying Cloud.* This resulted in a report that showed business managers and sales people how to take advantage of the fact that pockets of prosperity can be discovered and tapped into, no matter how good or bad business conditions may be. I called this investment strategy Business Cycle Management (BCM). Since then, that original report has been followed by other reports, articles, and speeches.

Chris, I have seen so many good people badly hurt by the government's manipulation of the **economy**, and I don't want it to happen to you. As a minor you are not in a position now to apply BCM to your own financial life, for the simple reason that you are too young to have much of one. However, it is crucially important that you begin to incorporate the BCM model into your daily way of looking at the world around you, especially the business world. If you can accomplish this now, you'll be ahead of the millions of adults who haven't a clue what is happening to them, and light years ahead of your peers. When you reach the age when you no longer have your parents' protection against the **boom-and-bust business cycle**, you will have the knowledge to protect yourself. Most people wander through their careers and financial lives totally at the mercy of this cycle. If they understood the story of the *Flying Cloud,* they'd be a lot better off.

Business Cycle Management is based on an economic process called the **injection effect**. The injection effect was touched on in my previous letters.[3] It is the change that occurs on Wall Street (the financial world) and Main Street (where most of us live and work) when the government injects new money into the economy.

By understanding Business Cycle Management, you can learn how to benefit from the injection effect rather than be hurt by it.

Some would say the injection effect and BCM cannot be explained without using a lot of calculus. I will give it a try by using historical examples and illustrations. A picture is worth a thousand words, I hope.

Chris, this might be a good time for you to review our prior correspondence about economics.[4] Pay particular

---

[3] Ibid.

[4] See Richard Maybury's books: WHATEVER HAPPENED TO PENNY CANDY? (about economics), and THE MONEY MYSTERY (more about velocity), published by Bluestocking Press, web site: www.BluestockingPress.com.

attention to letters seven and eight to refresh your knowledge of **business cycles**, and the terms **money supply**, **velocity**, and **money demand**. It will only take a few minutes and will make what I'm about to explain in my next few letters easier to understand, since what's to come will be a continuation of our prior discussions.

The difference between what you previously read and what you are about to read is **theory** versus **application**. You got the theory last time, and now you'll get more, but also a lot of the application.

I'll write again in a couple of days, after you have had time to dig out those letters and review them. Until then, remember that the injection effect is an economic process — it is the change that occurs on Wall Street and Main Street when the government injects new money into the economy. Business Cycle Management is the strategy to cope with, and prosper from, these injections.

I need to cover a few more preliminary facts, then in my sixth letter we will return to the story of the *Flying Cloud.*

As usual, I will be giving you a viewpoint you are not likely to get anywhere else, the non-statist viewpoint. Virtually everything to which you are exposed is **statist**[5], and if you don't get the other side of the story from me you will probably never get it. Few people talk about what's *really* happening when government officials change their **laws** and policies. Millions of people go through their whole lives never realizing there is another side, and this leaves them vulnerable to the forces we will be discussing in these letters.

Uncle Eric

---

[5] The statist and non-statist viewpoints are explained in the book ARE YOU LIBERAL? CONSERVATIVE? OR CONFUSED? by Richard J. Maybury, published by Bluestocking Press, web site: www.BluestockingPress.com.

2

Ethics and the Flood Of Data

Dear Chris,

The first two points to cover in our discussion of the injection effect and Business Cycle Management are (1) the ethics of BCM and (2) the deluge of business information that threatens to engulf us today. First, the ethics.

BCM takes advantage of the injection effect, and the injection effect hurts millions. Is it wrong to prosper from something that is harmful to others?

Yes, if you have control over this something. If you are ever in a position to stop the government's injections of money, I hope you will do so.

However, what if you have no more control over the injections of money than you do over a hurricane or earthquake? What if this process is simply part of your environment and all you are trying to do is cope with it, to get along as best you can?

Is it wrong to go into the business of building homes in an area that has been hit by an earthquake or hurricane? Would you be taking unfair advantage of someone? Of course not.

Some would disagree, they see the economy as a **zero sum game**. This means they think the amount of **wealth** is fixed. For one person to have more, another must have less. If I earn $10, then you or someone else must have lost it.

This confuses **money** with wealth. Wealth is goods and services — food, clothing, haircuts, cars, TVs, homes, and everything else that makes life better. Money is just the tool we use to measure and trade wealth. As long as a person has plenty of wealth, money is a minor consideration.

The economy is not a zero sum game. The amount of wealth can be increased — and people do this constantly, by working — so one person can have more without another having less. There is nothing wrong with becoming more prosperous *as long as you are not harming someone else.* In fact, it is your responsibility to accrue enough wealth so that you, and any dependents you may someday have, will not be a burden to society.

But I must caution you. Once you use BCM, you will earn wealth from the injection effect, and you may be tempted to see the injection effect as a good thing. You might even want it to continue and grow.

I want your solemn promise that you will do all you can to avoid this temptation. Continually remind yourself that the injection effect is evil, and help others understand how it affects them. Never do anything that would preserve or increase the injection effect. Adapt to it, but go no further than that.

Now for the second point, about the deluge of information. Thanks to the miraculous advances in computer sciences over the past several decades, the price of information is declining rapidly and it is fast approaching zero. Unemployment data, stock prices, election results, income distributions, weather forecasts, baseball scores, the flow of ocean currents, locations of oil deposits in Kazakhstan — the typical American now has access to all this and a lot more, all of it free or nearly so.

No one could possibly read even one percent of this information, so the question to answer is, "What should we pay attention to, and what should we ignore?"

That, I believe, will be one of the biggest challenges of the next several decades — sorting and prioritizing information.

Remember my explanation of models.[6] Models help us sort and prioritize information.

For instance, suppose you are watching a football game. The announcer says the quarterback's pass completion average is 66%, his speed in the hundred-yard dash is 10.1 seconds, and his hat size is 7. Which of the three statistics are important; which should you ignore?

The first two are important, ignore the third.

How do you know to ignore his hat size?

You know how football works. You know the rules of the game, the objective — to move the ball across the goal line — and the way plays are run.

In other words, you have in your mind a **model** of how the game works. This model tells you a quarterback's pass completions and speed are important to the outcome of the game but his hat size isn't.

Chris, by the time you finish reading this series of letters, you will have a more complete model of how the economy works. This model will tell you what information is important and what is not.

---

[6] See UNCLE ERIC TALKS ABOUT PERSONAL, CAREER AND FINANCIAL SECURITY, revised edition (2004) by Richard J. Maybury, published by Bluestocking Press, web site: www.BluestockingPress.com.

In fact, you will be so good at sorting information that you will be able to take a casual walk through a city and see a great deal that most of the people who live there do not recognize as important. In many cases you will know more about their futures than they do.

I will end this letter with the reminder that no matter how much money you make by using BCM to adapt to the injection effect, the injection effect itself remains a terribly evil thing. I hope you will do all you can to warn people about it.

Also, your models are your most valuable tool in knowing what information is important and what is not.

Uncle Eric

3

Hot Spots and Evidence

Dear Chris,

I'm glad you took the time to review our prior letters about economics. Before we get to the story of the *Flying Cloud*, however, some additional background and history will be helpful. Let's look at the period 1970 to 1990 and the 1987 stock market crash.

We subtract price increases from money supply increases to get the **"real" money supply**. As the chart shows, in 1970 the real money supply was $1,400 billion, and by 1990 it had risen to $2,500 billion,[7] but not steadily. Pauses in money supply growth brought recessions.

When the **Federal Reserve**[8] **(the Fed)** began increasing the money supply to end the 1982 recession, it sowed the seeds of a new monetary crisis. The supply of dollars increased, and the value of each individual dollar fell.

---

[7] Using the measure of money supply called M2.

[8] The Federal Reserve System is the central bank of the U.S. Its primary purpose is to control short-term interest rates and the supply of money. It is called "the Fed" for short. "Tightening" means restricting the money supply, which drives up short-term interest rates. "Loosening" means expanding the money supply, which causes short-term rates to fall. This is because interest is the price of renting money. When the supply is tight the price rises. When it's loose, the price falls.

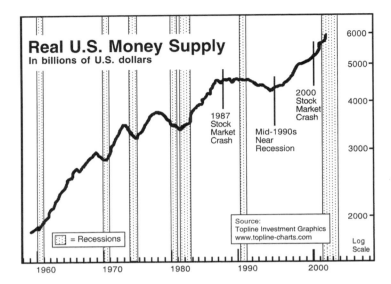

Real U.S. Money Supply
In billions of U.S. dollars

1987 Stock Market Crash

Mid-1990s Near Recession

2000 Stock Market Crash

Source:
Topline Investment Graphics
www.topline-charts.com

= Recessions

6000
5000
4000
3000
2000
Log Scale

1960 1970 1980 1990 2000

The "real" money supply is the money supply minus changes in prices. In this chart we use the M2 measure of money supply, and the index of consumer prices, to estimate the real money supply.

Recessions tend to occur just after the real money supply goes flat or falls.

The 2001 recession was an exception. During the 1990s, newly created dollars flowed mostly into only two areas, high-tech industries and the stock market. So, the recession was severe only in those areas. Also, this mildness probably reflected the fact that increases in the real money supply paused only slightly in the late 1990s.

By 1986, international investors had begun losing confidence in the stability of the dollar. Many no longer wanted it, so its value in international currency markets was falling. If you were traveling abroad and needed to exchange your U.S. dollars for a given amount of German marks, Swiss francs, or some other foreign currency, each month you needed more dollars to do it. Foreigners were afraid to accept the U.S.

dollar and demanded more to compensate for the risk that the value would fall further.

In 1987, to protect the dollar, the Federal Reserve began restricting the growth of the money supply. This triggered the 1987 stock market crash and later the 1990 recession.

The 1990 recession was not especially severe in terms of the number of people who lost their jobs, but by December 1991 it had become a political issue. Among the voters, President George (Herbert Walker) Bush's job approval rating was falling. The 1992 elections were approaching, and the Federal Reserve was coming under growing pressure to re-inflate us into an economic boom.

On December 20, 1992, the Federal Reserve cut the **discount rate**[9] a full percent to 3.5%, signaling that re-inflation had begun. Investment advisors all over the country began issuing buy recommendations, and the stock market shot upward.

What I'm about to tell you next, Chris, is very important. You must understand that new money does not descend on the economy in a uniform blanket as many economists and advisors assume. It is injected into specific locations, and it spreads outward *unevenly* from these locations. Some areas are flooded with new money and others receive none.

The points of injection become **hot spots** that offer business, career, and investment opportunities, but these new hot spots are not always easy to predict or identify. Spots that were hot in the past may not be in the future. The purpose of Business Cycle Management is to help you find and profit from these hot spots.

---

[9] The discount rate is an interest rate and one of the Federal Reserve's tools for manipulating the money supply. A rising rate means a restricted money supply, and a falling rate means a rising money supply.

Most analysts assume new money descends on the economy in a uniform blanket.

But the money is injected into specific locations, creating hot spots. It spreads outward from there.

Key point: Look for **evidence,** not **forecasts.**
For instance, suppose you are looking to buy **shares of stock** in a well-run company, and your broker tells you XYZ Company is expected to do very well in the future because it has entered an especially promising hot spot. He points to all the new employees that have been hired and the new buildings and equipment XYZ has purchased. Do you buy XYZ?

No, not until you see the company's *sales.* That's the key, sales. *Sales* tell you if the company is actually getting some of this new money.

And as long as you own the stock or work for the firm, watch sales. When they drop off, be ready to bail out, the flow of money has weakened.

Don't be misled into thinking the flow will continue forever. It might recover and grow again, but all good things come to an end eventually.

During the 1990s, an unknown but certainly very large portion of the Federal Reserve's injections of new money went into the stock market. This caused the largest stock market boom in history. From 1992 to 1997, the money supply increased 425 billion dollars[10] and the stock market rose more than 100%.[11] Many people became convinced that "this time it's different," the boom would go on for decades without a serious drop. It was as if all the money supply declines and stock market crashes of the past had never happened. Ignoring the lessons of history, people who knew nothing about the stock market poured their retirement nest eggs and children's college money into it.

Chris, on many occasions I have discussed **standards of proof** and demanding evidence before investing money.

---

[10] Again using the measure of money supply called M2.
[11] The Dow Jones Industrial Average.

I wrote you about this in a prior set of letters.[12] If you have these handy, now is a good time to read them again.

Speaking of investments, here's a good rule of thumb. When lots of people who know nothing about something are buying it, that's a good time to sell it. The reason is that the last people to get into an investment are those who know nothing about it. When they are in, there is no one else left to buy, so the **price** cannot go much higher.

Also, remember that in a **bull market** (a strongly rising market) even a simpleton looks smart; he can buy anything and the price will go up. When you go in search of investment advice, try to get it from someone who has done well in a **bear market** (a falling market).

Until my next letter, Chris, remember that the Federal Reserve's injections of money go into specific areas, and these areas become hot spots, but no hot spot lasts forever. Always demand *evidence* of the flow of money before you try to tap into it, and be ready to bail out when the flow stops.

Uncle Eric

---

12 Uncle Eric is referring to his letter titled "The Most Important Question to Ask for the Rest of Your Life," in Richard Maybury's book UNCLE ERIC TALKS ABOUT PERSONAL, CAREER & FINANCIAL SECURTIY, revised edition (2004) published by Bluestocking Press, web site: www.BluestockingPress.com.

4

Austrian Economics

Dear Chris,

You are right, the examples I am using in this series of letters are drawn mostly from the period 1970 to 1990. These decades contained three full economic cycles including the worst recession since the Great Depression. We are far enough removed from them now that we can study them with the clarity of hindsight. The next recession after that of 1990-91 did not happen until 2001. This ten years was the longest boom in American history. It was so unusual that we will probably need at least another ten years, and one or two more recessions to study, before we can get a clear picture of what has been happening. My suspicion is that velocity[13] has become the dominant force causing changes. I also suspect velocity became very erratic, especially after September 11, 2001[14]. Time will tell.

---

[13] See Maybury's books WHATEVER HAPPENED TO PENNY CANDY? and THE MONEY MYSTERY, published by Bluestocking Press.

[14] On September 11, 2001, in an attack against the United States, over 3000 civilians were murdered. The World Trade Center in New York was destroyed, as well as a portion of the Pentagon. Four civilian airliners were destroyed, including their passengers and crew. This attack is also referred to as Sept. 11, Sept. 11 Attack, and 9-11.

Don't be fooled by the many get-rich-quick hot tips you see advertised. What I'm about to provide you is a serious explanation of the monetary forces that cause hot and **cold spots** in the economy and how to prosper from the hot spots without getting burned.

I don't believe you will ever forget this model, Chris. For the rest of your life it will be one of your most important tools for making career, business, and investment decisions. You will see and understand vastly more than any of your friends. In fact, I'm sure you will see and understand more than some of the top managers of Fortune 500 companies.

How can I be so confident that little of what I am about to tell you is understood by managers of top corporations?

Few of today's business people have studied the free-market **Austrian economics** of Nobel Laureate F.A. Hayek and his teacher Ludwig von Mises.[15] They've studied only **Keynesian** or **Monetarist** economics, and these brands do not contain an explanation of the injection effect.

For a while in the early 1980s, Austrian economics received a lot of attention because it was popular with Britain's Prime Minister Margaret Thatcher and her advisors, but they are out of office now, and few business people retain an interest in Austrian economics.

Don't believe it? Test it yourself. Every time you meet a business person ask him or her about Austrian economics, Hayek, Mises and the injection effect. I'll bet not more than one in a hundred will have the foggiest idea what you are talking about. The U.S. Government uses Keynesian and

---

[15] "Austrian" because the founders were from Austria. Most "Austrian" economists are Americans. For a more thorough explanation see WHATEVER HAPPENED TO PENNY CANDY? by Richard J. Maybury, published by Bluestocking Press, web site: www.BluestockingPress.com.

Monetarist economics, so this is what is taught in the colleges. Colleges get a lot of government money.

This isn't to say I think Monetarist economics is totally without merit. I think the Monetarists have some great insights, perhaps the best of which is velocity, but the Austrian model seems to me to be the one that best fits the facts. In other words, it's the one that most clearly explains the economic history of the past six thousand years.

However, I have made this observation. Like other economic models, the Austrian model was created by theoreticians who were trying to understand how the world works. They had little interest in practical applications for you and me.

So, for those of us who must live and work in the real world, the injection effect concept is a bit rough and misleading. It gives a picture of the government *forcing* money into the economy. In reality, the government only offers the money. Firms and individuals accept it and spend it. As they spend it, the money flows outward through a network of *voluntary* transactions. Nowhere is the money actually injected, it is poured.

The *unpredictability* of this pouring causes waves of windfall profits for some people, and waves of bankruptcies for others.

To avoid the mistakes that could occur from the assumption the money is forced in, I use the metaphor of pitchers and **cones**, which I will explain in letters to come. I also use lots of illustrations; they are much easier to remember and use than mathematical calculations.

Why is Austrian economics different? Most economists and investment advisors assume the economy is a giant machine. Some speak of the economy accelerating or slowing down, others of it heating up or cooling off.

Easiest Places to Make Sales

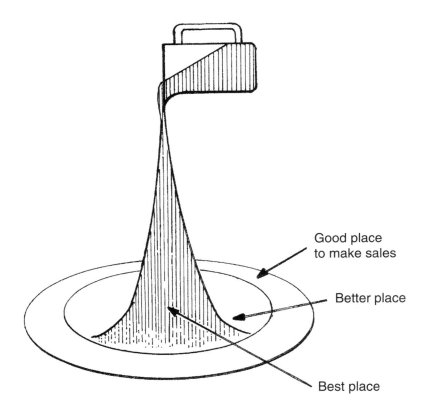

Good place
to make sales

Better place

Best place

The tops of the cones are the best places to make sales. As jewelers, luxury car dealers, and swimming pool builders discover, this is where money is most plentiful. Here money demand tends to be lower and velocity higher.

One way to find these areas is to ask jewelers, luxury car dealers, and pool builders who their best customers are.

The Austrian school points out that the economy is not hardware or buildings — it is living, breathing, biological organisms — people. The Austrian economist sees the economy not as a machine but as an **ecology.**

In other words, Austrians see the economy the way marketing managers do. Marketing managers know they are not studying things, they are studying human behavior.

Incidentally, marketing managers rarely look at the big picture, they look for niches. Few know that they are trying to locate the hot spots created by the injection effect.

Chris, next I will say a few words about how businesses are organized, then we will get into the story of the *Flying Cloud*. Until then, remember that I'm using free-market "Austrian" economics. This is the only type of economics that has done a thorough investigation of the injection effect.[16]

Uncle Eric

---

[16] These investigations can be found in many of the works of economists F.A. Hayek and Ludwig von Mises. The place to start is Mises' THEORY OF MONEY AND CREDIT published in 1912. (Be warned, it's heavy reading.) Neither Irving Fisher nor John Maynard Keynes, probably the most highly regarded economists of their day, saw the 1930s Great Depression coming, but Hayek and Mises did.

5

Line and Staff

Dear Chris,

Every business enterprise performs two primary functions, sales and production. These are the **line functions**.

All other parts of the firm — accounting, finance, legal, personnel, administration, etc. — are support for the line. These supports are the **staff functions**.

The **production function** of a butcher is to purchase sides of beef and cut them into small pieces. The **sales function** is to wait on customers who walk in off the street.

The production function of a TV station is to create or buy programs containing time-slots for commercials. The sales function is to sell this commercial time.

A real estate developer makes houses that are sold to home buyers.

At first glance some businesses do not appear to have production or sales functions, but look closer. Consider a bank. What is its production function?

A bank appears not to have one, but it does; it gathers money. This money is then lent or rented to borrowers — that's the sales function.

Flow Chart of a Business

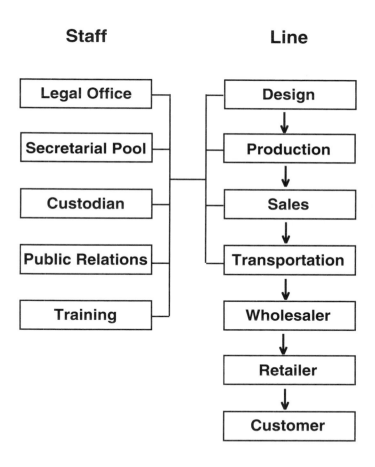

Staff

Line

Staff	Line
Legal Office	Design
Secretarial Pool	Production
Custodian	Sales
Public Relations	Transportation
Training	Wholesaler
	Retailer
	Customer

Next consider retailers. Their production function is the gathering and storage of merchandise. This is why a store is called a **store**, it is a storage place for goods awaiting sale.

The line functions are the reason for a firm's existence and they must perform well. If not, the battle is lost no matter how well the staff might do. All my letters will deal with line functions.

The line and staff functions apply to your home and family, too. Your parents' work is the production function. They trade their work for money, this is the sales function.

They also have a checking account, they follow a budget and a calendar of appointments, and do a lot of other things that are support for the line. These are the staff functions. I know you perform one of the staff functions, Chris, because you've told me you mow the lawn for your parents so that they don't need to. Mowing the lawn is not absolutely necessary for earning a living, so it's not a line function, but it is helpful, so it's a staff function.

Most of Business Cycle Management deals with the sales end of the line, and that's what we will get into first. That's the Clipper Ship Strategy. Later I'll deal with the production end.

Some of these ideas may not seem immediately useful, but in most cases this will be because all the pieces of the puzzle are not yet in place. By the time you get to the end of these letters the picture will be complete.

As you read along, underline every idea that appears useful to you. Afterwards, let my letters sit for a week or two to let these ideas simmer, then reread them. You will find more useful ideas because you will be able to see many interrelationships that were not apparent on the first reading.

The economy is an organic system where all parts are connected to all other parts, the opportunities to profit from these connections are limitless.

As we shall see, there is little here that is new. For centuries business managers, workers, and investors have been accidently discovering bits and pieces of Business Cycle Management. They have been stumbling onto sales and production techniques that worked, seldom realizing *why* they worked. All I've done is compile these off-the-shelf techniques into a coherent, unified whole. Millions of people are already doing some of these things but don't realize it because they don't have the so-called big picture.

Chris, next I will introduce you to the most important part of Business Cycle Management; I call it the **Clipper Ship Strategy**. It's a way to learn from history, and I think you will find it fascinating. It's about the *Flying Cloud* and her sister ships.

Until then, remember that all businesses and homes have line and staff functions. The line functions are the heart of the enterprise, and they are the focus of my letters about Business Cycle Management.

Uncle Eric

6

The Clipper Ship Strategy

Dear Chris,

Perhaps the most important off-the-shelf technique for dealing with the injection effect was discovered by owners of clipper ships during the 1800s. The story takes a few minutes to tell but once told it will be cemented in your mind and much easier to use than the hundreds of pages of economic charts and formulas it demonstrates.

The clipper was a long, slender transport[17] vessel with a sharp, long prow. Copied from the design of French warships, it was built for speed. It had three masts slanting slightly backwards and rigged with every inch of sail the designers could cram onto them.

For a cargo ship, a clipper's hold was small. Made of oak and other hardwoods, it was expensive to build. But for a time, the clipper was one of the most profitable types of ships in operation and it was constructed in large numbers. From 1848 to 1852, 160 were built in the United States alone.

---

[17] A vehicle used for hauling cargo or passengers. Usually refers to ships or planes.

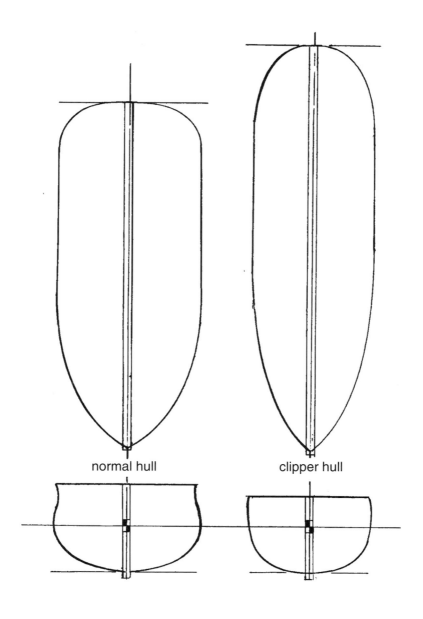

normal hull   clipper hull

Why? What would cause ship owners and builders to go on a crash program to make ships that had such a high construction cost and limited cargo capacity? What's more, why would they do so during the 1840s when the country was in a **depression**?

The answer is that prices and profits were high on the west coast and low on the east coast. Money could be earned by quickly transporting cargo from east to west. Few of the ship owners and builders understood all the economics behind this, but they didn't need to. All they needed was to see the difference in prices and to respond to this difference. They were following the signals of the market.

For us, their example becomes useful and profitable if we do look into the economics behind the clipper ship industry. The story begins with the California gold rush.

In 1848 gold was discovered in California and tens of thousands of people migrated west. When they arrived in the gold fields they found plenty of gold — plenty of money — but little else. There was a shortage of almost every necessity known to man.

In other words, in California huge amounts of money were chasing small amounts of goods. At the going rate of $16 per ounce for gold, a pair of boots cost $30 — almost two ounces of gold. In today's terms this was more than $700.

An onion cost a dollar, equal to $22 today. A pound of potatoes, $1.50, or $33 today.

A month's rent for a small hotel room was equal to the price of a new house back east.

In a restaurant in the gold rush town of Mokelumne Hill, a single slice of bread cost a dollar; buttered, two dollars, or $44 today.

Indeed, most goods were so scarce and the difficulty of hauling them into the gold fields so great that in parts of California the nature of the goods themselves had little to do with the price. In Sonora, all merchandise sold at a uniform $3 per pound regardless of what it was.

Tools, of course, were in great demand. Shovels and picks arriving in San Francisco were marked up 1500 percent. (Figure it out, Chris. Using today's dollars, suppose a shovel cost $12.00 on the depressed east coast. If a merchant bought a thousand, shipped them to San Francisco, and sold them to people who were willing to pay 1500 percent more than the east coast price, how much profit did he make? The answer is at the end of this letter.)

The miners had the money to pay these prices. At Drytown in 1848 it was common for a miner to dig out six ounces of gold each day. In today's terms this would be an income of more than $2100 per day.

In other words, California was a huge pile of money in search of goods to buy, at a time when the east coast was a huge manufacturing center in a depressed condition, short of cash and ready to produce goods at low prices.

The two coasts of the United States were rather like two sealed tanks, one highly pressurized and the other containing a vacuum. Ship owners realized that if the two could be linked, the deluge of money flowing east through the pipeline would be enormous. Anyone who tapped into this flow would quickly be able to skim off enough to become very wealthy.

Some also realized that the disparity in pressure would not last forever. Once the connection was made, the tanks would begin to equalize. Whatever was done to tap the flow would have to be done quickly.

The race was on to build the fastest merchant ships possible. No one paid much attention to cargo capacity since the California mark-up on goods was so great that only a small amount of cargo was needed to reap huge profits. What was important was speed. A merchant must get his goods to the gold fields fast before the easily accessible surface gold was depleted.

The first real clipper ship had been built in 1833. Over the years the design had been gradually improved, increasing the speed of the ships for the China tea trade. Tea had to be delivered to market fast before it spoiled.

The discovery of gold in California focused so much attention on speed that ship builders came out with the so-called extreme clipper. Very long and narrow, the extreme clipper was the fastest wind-driven cargo ship ever built. Sometimes they were called California clippers.

The *Flying Cloud* was the most extreme clipper ever designed. This is why it was able to make the trip from New York to San Francisco in a record 89 days. The *Flying Cloud* was 240 feet long and her top mast was 200 feet above the water. When her sails were spread full, they were 160 feet across — about the width of a football field.

It is hard to believe, but true, that extreme clippers did not reduce speed in darkness or bad weather. For them a storm was regarded as good news, the high winds made them even swifter. These maritime greyhounds often came into port with their sails and rigging in tatters from the pounding they took going full tilt through high seas.

The voyages through the frigid wind and water around Cape Horn were the most punishing. Imagine what it was like to be a crewman on a ship that didn't slow down for anything no matter how rough the weather. These men were well paid and greatly admired for their skill and daring.

An important point for us is that the extreme clippers ran their mad races to San Francisco and back for only three years. By 1851 the easily accessible surface gold was gone. Also, the pressure in the two tanks had begun to equalize. It looked like the era of the clipper was about to end. But here we come to the most instructive part of the clipper story.

A California gold-miner by the name of E. Hargraves had decided to go in search of a new gold field. He went to Australia, and, in February 1851, discovered gold there.

The Australian Gold Rush was on, and the fast clippers *diverted* from their San Francisco runs. They rushed south to this new cornucopia of money as the San Francisco run was turned over to the slower, larger ships.

The extreme clippers made the Australia run for another three years, until 1854 when the easily accessible Australian gold was depleted and freight rates had begun to decline. By 1855, extreme clippers were no longer economical and construction of them had ceased. The ship builders were creating broader, slower ships with much greater cargo capacities for the lower freight rates. These were called "modified clippers."

The story of the extreme clipper is important for us today because it demonstrates four important rules for achieving success:

1. Find out where there is a pile of money.
2. Tap into that pile.
3. Don't expect the pile to last forever.
4. Always be searching for new piles.

Today, of course, the piles of money aren't natural gold deposits, they are the government's artificial paper deposits (fiat paper money deposits). But the economic principles are the same. The key is speed. Get in fast, while the money is plentiful, and out before it is depleted. For it *will* be depleted — in today's economy there is no stability.

Chris, I hope you enjoyed the clipper ship story. In my next letter we will take a closer look at those piles of money.

Uncle Eric

P.S. Here is the answer to the shovel problem: A $12 shovel marked up 1500% would have had 1500% added to its price, for a total price of $192. The gross profit on the $12 shovel would have been $180. On a thousand shovels, $180,000. Imagine, $180,000 gross profit on a $12,000 load of shovels!

From this the merchant would have had to pay the shipping cost. I don't know how much that would have been, but the incentive, as you can see, was for the merchant to get the shovels to California as quickly as possible, then get the money back to New York equally as fast so that even more shovels could be purchased and shipped west, and so on. The faster the profits could be sent to New York the faster more shovels could be sent to California.

7

Piles of Money

Dear Chris,

As I mentioned in an earlier letter, when discussing **inflation**, many economists and business forecasters seem to assume the newly created money descends on the economy in a uniform blanket, as if it were sprayed from a giant crop-duster aircraft flying coast to coast. This assumption leads to an image of prices rising uniformly all over the country in response to this descending blanket of money.

This assumption is wrong. The newly created money does not descend on the economy in a uniform blanket. The belief that it does can lead to all kinds of disastrous business, career, and investment decisions, and it can cause us to pass up many opportunities.

The government does not give the newly created money to everyone uniformly for the simple reason that it does not want everyone to have the money. It wants certain specific individuals and firms to have the money. In many cases these are people who helped get someone elected to office or who promise to help get someone elected.

This means the money is poured into the economy in specific locations. Then, as the recipients of the money at these locations receive it, they spend it and thereby begin spreading it throughout the economy.

Form this picture in your mind: The money enters the economy as if it were a thick fluid, like molasses, poured from thousands of pitchers — thousands of government spending programs. Imagine each dollar being a molecule of the fluid.

At the points of entry, the money, or molasses, piles up; it forms deep spots, which you can imagine as inverted cones.

All kinds of firms and individuals crowd into these cones, as the fictional record shop did in my economic letter to you about wheelbarrows and recessions.[18]

In his fine book A TIME FOR TRUTH, former Treasury Secretary William E. Simon describes the process: "More than 60 million Americans now get some kind of check from the

---

[18] See chapter titled "Wallpapers, Wheelbarrows and Recessions" in WHATEVER HAPPENED TO PENNY CANDY? published by Bluestocking Press, web site: www.BluestockingPress.com.

Cones of Money Cause
Hot Spots in the Economy

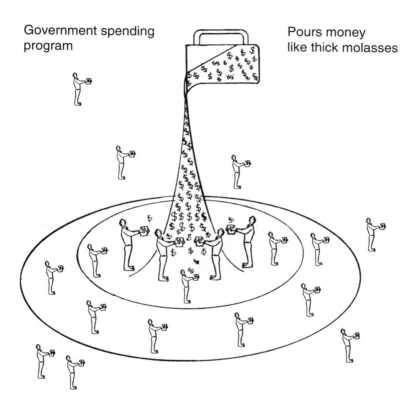

Government spending
program

Pours money
like thick molasses

Government officials pour money into the economy. Firms and individuals gather at the entry points to catch as much of this money as they can.

As the recipients spend it, the money flows outward like thick molasses filling a bathtub.

These entry points are hot spots where sales are easier to make because money is plentiful.

*Fed stands for Federal Reserve or Central Bank Printing Press.

government. They gather beneath the federal faucet. They agree that it pours forth a torrent and that the handle appears to be missing. But rather than summon a plumber, they jockey for position beneath the stream with buckets, pans and cups."[19]

As these firms and individuals receive and spend the money, the money flows outward from the cones and gradually raises the money supply and prices throughout the economy, as if the molasses were filling a bathtub.

Prices rise in a sort of wave expanding outward from the point of entry. The people who are first in line to get the money are able to spend it *before* prices rise, and those who are last in line are not able to spend it until *after* prices rise.

Note that prices rise first, fastest, and highest at the entry points of the money because this is where the supply of money is greatest — as in 1848 California. For you, the people and organizations in these areas who are among the early recipients of the money are likely to be very good customers, employers, or investments.

Those who are not among the early recipients are hurt badly because their incomes do not rise as fast as prices rise. Trying to establish some kind of career, business, or investment relationship with them can be a waste of time and energy.

Chris, in my next letter I'll hook velocity into this explanation of the cones. Until then, remember that as the money pours into the economy it forms cones or hot spots where the money is most plentiful; it spreads outward from there.

Uncle Eric

---

[19] A TIME FOR TRUTH by William E. Simon published by Reader's Digest Press, a division of McGraw Hill Book Co., 1978. Out of Print.

The Great Drought Deluge

The 1988 drought was a disaster for Midwestern grain growers. TV news reports showed thousands of acres of shriveled cornstalks and cracked, dusty fields. To help these farmers, Congress enacted the 1988 drought relief program.

At each step of the legislative process the program was broadened until farmers in every state except Hawaii were collecting "drought" relief. A $3.9 billion deluge of money poured onto the farms.

In a 1989 study the Associated Press[20] discovered that about one-quarter of all U.S. farmers received money not only for drought damage but for normal operating losses due to insects, sand, wind, cold, fungus, and even "ineffective herbicide." In one California county the money was doled out for "anything related to nature."

---

[20] "Farmers Get Drought Windfall," SACRAMENTO BEE, December 11, 1989, p.1.

8

The Money Spreads

Dear Chris,

In the early stages of an inflation the money takes a long time, sometimes years, to spread to its maximum limits. You can envision the money (molasses) at this stage as being cool and spreading slowly. As explained in my prior letters on economics, the velocity of circulation is low.

In later stages, the people have become wise to what is happening, and they are spending the money as fast as they can. They know it loses value as they hold it. This is what was happening during the financial panic of 1980 and I expect it to happen again.

In these later stages the money is very hot — its velocity is high — and it is spreading rapidly, pushing up prices very quickly. If it is not cooled, a **hyperinflation** will occur.

Governments try to delay the onset of hyperinflation for as long as possible, so they sometimes allow their pitchers (spending programs) to become empty. The money stops pouring in some places, as it did in the example of the record shop mentioned in my previous set of letters on economics.

The people in these places are left high and dry. They are stuck with commitments to pay rents, interest, utility bills, insurance premiums, and other types of fixed **overhead**[21] without enough income to cover these costs. They go broke, never understanding the real reason: they were lured into a cone of money without realizing the cone was only *temporary*.

This is what happened to American farmers during the 1970s and 1980s. In the 1970s they were living in cones, and in the 1980s the cones went dry. During the 1970s the government had been expanding the money supply, and part of this money flowed onto the farms through the Agriculture Department's loan and **subsidy** programs. Money was plentiful and the farmers were borrowing it to expand their operations.

Another part of the money supply flowed into the **commodity markets** where farm goods are bought and sold. This drove up the prices of farm goods, pouring even more money into the pockets of the farmers.

These high prices deceived the farmers into thinking they would always be able to make the payments on the money they were borrowing.

Then during the early 1980s, Federal Reserve officials, worried about the falling value of the dollar, reduced the flow of money. Prices of farm products dropped and the farmers were unable to meet their payments.

Chris, in my next letter I'll say a few words about how law affects cones. Until then, remember, never assume a cone will last forever. Like a clipper ship, always be ready to sail away to a new cone.

Uncle Eric

---

[21] Overhead is a rather nebulous term which generally refers to costs that are not directly attributable to the product and are not easily cut back. Opposite of variable cost. In automobile production, steel is a variable cost, and the fire insurance on the factory is overhead.

9

Cones and Sales

Dear Chris,

Suppose you own a business. What do you think will be one of the most effective ways for a firm to profit in a government-controlled economy?

A firm should locate one of the pitchers of money and place itself so that it is standing directly beneath the pitcher, right?

Right. Unfortunately.

This does not necessarily mean you should apply for some kind of government contract or subsidy. You might do that, millions do, or you might prefer to keep a distance from the government.

If you'd rather keep a distance, don't get directly beneath the cone, but get close, find a way to sell to the people who are getting those contracts or subsidies.

Or, if that's still too close for your tastes, step back a bit further and sell to those who are selling to the recipients of the contracts and subsidies. Or step back even further...

You get my point. You will tap into some kind of cone somehow, it's virtually inescapable. The choice about how close you get to the pitcher is entirely yours. But always remember that the cone will not last forever.

Unfortunately, few managers know anything of cones. Once they find themselves in a spot where money is flowing heavily, they organize the firm's plant and equipment on the assumption this flow will continue. When it stops, the firm goes broke.

This is one reason everyone needs to understand such "philosophical" issues as **political power**, law, and history. *Everyone* needs to understand the nature and behavior of government — it's the most important force affecting a person's wallet. It's more important than customers, more important than employees, more important than anyone or anything.

For most people their single biggest expenditure is taxes. It's more than food, more than housing, more than anything.

Business people who lack political savvy often find a hot spot and talk themselves into believing this hot spot will go on and on. Be constantly aware that **political law** can change at any time without warning, which means the flow of money can change without warning. A twenty year-old hot spot can go cold overnight. Remember the discussions we had in prior letters about political law.[22] The economy — in your case meaning your career, business, or investments — cannot be stable if the law is not stable.

Your success in business will depend heavily on your knowing how close you are to a cone of money and how dependent you are on this cone. This means you must know where your money comes from.

---

[22] Uncle Eric is referring to WHATEVER HAPPENED TO JUSTICE? by Richard J. Maybury, published by Bluestocking Press, web site: www.BluestockingPress.com.

Chris, in my next letter I will talk about the opposite of cones, which I call **sinkholes**. This will further refine your model of how the economy works and how to prosper in it.

Until then, remember that for the rest of your life your financial success will depend very much on your ability to answer the question: Who are the buyers of my goods or services and where do they get their money?

Uncle Eric

10

Scooping and Pouring

Dear Chris,

Not all the money in the cones is newly created. Most is old money that has been in the economy for a long time. The government scoops it out, in the form of **tax** collections, and mixes it with the newly created money.

The scooping (tax collection) process tends to leave an area economically depressed wherever more money is scooped out than is poured back in. The people in these sinkholes are economic martyrs, but they seldom know why because they understand little about economics.

In December 1982 — which was the bottom of the worst recession since the Great Depression — unemployment among farm workers was 16.3%, construction workers, 21.6%, and manufacturing workers, 14.2%. Among government workers it was a mere 5.1%.

That's a demographic picture. For a geographic picture, we can look at California in the 1991 recession. In March of that year, unemployment in Plumas County was 20.7%, in Tulare County, 21.6%, and Colusa County, 23.8%. In Sacramento County, where the state government was headquartered, unemployment was only 6.9%.

The Business Landscape of Cones and Sinkholes

The people's wealth is not always located where government officials wish it to be. Officials change the locations of the wealth by scooping money from one area and pouring it into another.

> The government has no wealth of its own. Anything received from Washington must first be sent to Washington.

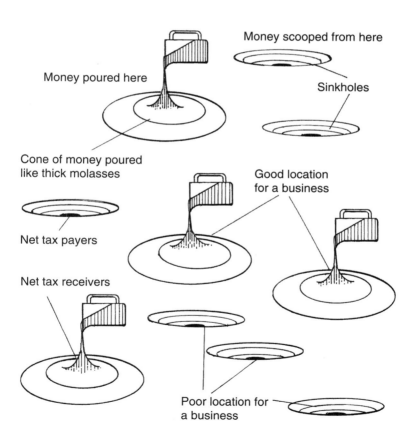

Very few of the cones or sinkholes are stable. Their locations change constantly, the reason being that political activism has become the national religion.

Everybody wants to be in a cone and nobody wants to be in a sinkhole.

People who find themselves in depressed areas may not know how or why they got there, but they do know how to complain about it loudly. Politicians who are trying to win votes must either create new cones over the depressed areas or move existing cones away from old areas where the voters have become complacent. The cones dance all over the landscape.

If you watch the news media closely, you will find reports of this process in action. Some years ago, U.S. NEWS & WORLD REPORT[23] ran an article disclosing that of the 435 congressional districts in the country, 115 got more money in military spending than they paid out in taxes. Said U.S. NEWS, "Losers include districts in Illinois, New York, Michigan, Pennsylvania and Ohio. Winners: California, Virginia, Missouri, Connecticut, Washington. If the Pentagon continues to concentrate its spending in fewer districts, it will further erode support for major military outlays."

As this last comment implies, government spending frequently occurs not because someone *needs* something but because they want a cone of money created over them. The purchase of weapons, schools, highways, hospitals, and all kinds of other government goods and services is often (always?) due not to a careful evaluation of costs vs. benefits but to the fact that military contractors, doctors, teachers,

---

[23] August 27, 1984.

construction companies, and others happen to be "politically active."

Efforts to persuade apathetic and uninformed voters to go to the polls during elections often amount to little more than thinly disguised efforts to change or protect the locations of the cones.

In short, the cones and depressions come and go because the squeaky wheel gets the grease. To be successful in a government-controlled economy, *follow the **dancing cones!***

But never allow yourself to become dependent on a cone that is not squeaking, its life span will be short.

Chris, in my next letter we will talk more about law and cones. Until then, remember that the cones are not stable, they dance.

Uncle Eric

11

All Roads

Dear Chris,

All roads lead to Rome. We can now see how this popular expression developed. The Romans discovered that in a government-controlled economy no one survives unless he has "connections" in the government.[24] To be without political clout is to be without a cone.

I use a lot of ink writing about the 1982 recession because it was the worst since the Great Depression, it makes an excellent test case.

In 1985, officials were singing praises to the booming recovery from the 1982 recession, but not everyone was doing well. As the chart that follows shows, in 1985 an average family of four in Illinois suffered a net loss to the Federal Government of $4628, while a family in Maryland received a $3432 gain — a difference between the two families of $8060. In which state would you rather have been trying to sell your goods or services?

Notice how the unemployment rate was lower in the states with the net gains.

---

[24] For more information about Ancient Rome, see Richard Maybury's book ANCIENT ROME: HOW IT AFFECTS YOU TODAY, published by Bluestocking Press, web site: www.BluestockingPress.com.

Per Capita Profit & Loss, and Unemployment[25]

State	Per Capita Federal Tax Collections	Per Capita Federal Input	Per Capita Profit/Loss	Unemployment
Maryland	$ 3461	$ 4319	+ 858	4.6%
Illinois	3373	2216	- 1157	9.0
Oregon	2734	2448	- 286	8.8
Florida	2884	3027	+ 143	6.0
Arizona	2562	3005	+ 443	6.5

This is not to suggest a direct one-to-one connection between federal revenue flows and unemployment, other factors come into play. But taking money from people certainly does not help them.

We are now living in a country where all roads lead to Washington, D.C. because *political law determines the locations of the cones*, which means everyone is forced to compete for control of the law.[26]

As you might expect, the largest, most stable cone in the world is Washington, D.C. If you own a Washington, D.C. business or work for someone in Washington, D.C., you may not need to practice Business Cycle Management, your cone is virtually permanent.

In 1982, when the recession was at its worst and double-digit unemployment had struck almost every state, the unemployment rate in Washington, D.C. was a mere six percent and per capita income was higher than anywhere except Alaska.

---

[25] U.S NEWS & WORLD REPORT, April 15 and July 15, 1985 and STATISTICAL ABSTRACT OF THE U.S.

[26] For a thorough discussion of the relationship between political law and economic prosperity, read WHATEVER HAPPENED TO JUSTICE? by Richard J. Maybury, published by Bluestocking Press, web site: www.BluestockingPress.com.

It has long been so. William Simon: "In 1977, for example, the average income of a civilian employee of the Federal Government in the Washington, D.C. area was over $20,000 a year. The average income of taxpayers working in private industry was slightly over half of that — about $12,000."

Since you are deeply involved in your education, you might be interested in a study done in 1996.[27] The Heritage Foundation tracked the flow of school tax money from the taxpayers to Washington, D.C., then back to the schools in the taxpayers' neighborhoods. On average, for each dollar taken from the taxpayers, only 85¢ got back to the schools. The other 15¢ stayed in Washington, D.C. And the 85¢ was not distributed uniformly. I have picked ten states as examples. For each tax dollar taken, here is the per capita amount received:

Alaska	$3.12
Arizona	1.42
Colorado	0.58
Connecticut	0.39
Illinois	0.64
Montana	2.13
New Hampshire	0.47
New Mexico	2.34
Virginia	0.68
Wyoming	1.28

---

[27]   U.S. DEPARTMENT OF EDUCATION FINANCING OF ELEMENTARY AND SECONDARY EDUCATION: WHERE THE MONEY GOES, #126, December 30, 1996, Heritage Foundation, Washington, DC.

Going through the list of all 50 states, I found no relationship between the prosperity of the state and the amount it received. Incomes in Arizona and Colorado, for instance, were near the national average, and in Alaska about a third higher, but Arizona and Alaska both got a lot more tax money than Colorado. Apparently, the folks in Arizona and Alaska were more politically active, so those in Colorado were forced to subsidize them. If Coloradans retaliate, getting more deeply into politics than the other two, we can expect their take to increase.

If, in 1996, you had been earning your living selling goods or services to schools, which states would have been the ones to target first?

Incidentally, about that 15¢ that stays in Washington, governments are greedy. They are comprised of humans, and these humans have all the same vices everyone else has. The way a bureaucrat gets more money and prestige is by working his way to the top of a bureaucracy. Once there, he wants his bureaucracy to grow so that he has more responsibility and, therefore, justification for more pay.

In fact, if you research the behavior of governments over the past several thousand years, I think you will find that of all types of organizations, governments are the most greedy — which is a point of view you rarely hear.

As I have said, almost every source of information to which you are exposed has a statist slant, and if you do not get the other side of the story from me, you probably will not get it. By the way, Chris, here's an exercise for you. In one column list the *sources of information* on which you rely (i.e. newspapers, radio news, television news, magazines, teachers, librarians, authors, experts, consultants, etc.) Be very specific, listing the name of a particular newspaper, radio commentator, magazine, etc. In an adjacent column list any affiliation to government each of these sources of information may have. For example, do they receive government funding? Are they regulated by government? If a source is regulated or funded by government, do you think objectivity might be compromised in any way?

Back to cones, or hot spots. There are two types: demographic and geographic.

Federal government employees are **demographic hot spots**. They receive the money as individuals. Examples of other demographic hot spots are military retirees, police officers, and other state and local civil servants.

Geographic hot spots are areas — states, counties, cities, or neighborhoods — that receive large sums of money. Examples:

In the late 1980s, after all the effects of the 1982 recession were over, the national capitol, Washington, D.C., had a per capita income of $20,070 and an unemployment rate of 6.3% while New Orleans had a per capita income of only $12,838 and an unemployment rate of 10%.

While Youngstown, Ohio, had a per capita income of $12,364 and an unemployment rate of 9.7%, the state capitol, Columbus, Ohio, had a per capita income of $14,476 and an unemployment rate of only 5.4%, one of the best in the country.

Hot spots can be any size, from a single individual to a state. The way you envision them depends on your situation. If you are selling encyclopedias door to door, think of hot spots or cones as being individuals. If you are advertising cornflakes on national TV, your target hot spots can be state or county in size.

Chris, in my next letter I will say a bit more about the locations of cones. Until then, remember that cones can be either demographic or geographic.

Uncle Eric

12

Cone Creation

Dear Chris,

Finding cones is not difficult, the government makes no secret of the locations. In fact, the politicians and bureaucrats who create the cones brag about them. You've undoubtedly heard news reports such as: "In a news conference yesterday, Senator Humpty, a demublican from the state of Confusion,[28] announced the introduction of SB93, the Humpty Dumpty Bill. This bill will give a $50 million boost to the egg industry and create thousands of new jobs for all the king's horses and men."

The good senator carefully avoids mentioning that the $50 million will really not create any new jobs at all. It will only remove a few hundred jobs from each of a few hundred communities around the nation (the **net tax payers**[29]) and transfer these jobs to where the senator needs them to win the

---

[28] Demublicans and republicrats are referred to in the book ARE YOU LIBERAL, CONSERVATIVE OR CONFUSED? by Richard J. Maybury, published by Bluestocking Press, web site: www.BluestockingPress.com.

[29] A net tax receiver is a person who gets more from the government than he pays in taxes. A net tax payer is the opposite.

next election (**net tax receivers**). This was once called the old shell game, now it is called **fiscal policy**.

The making of fiscal policy can be a fascinating process to watch. Behind-the-scenes diplomacy among the nation's statesmen often sounds something like, "If you help me pour $10 million into the Ajax Bazooka Factory at Warprofits, Wyoming, I will help you pour $10 million into the Acme Values Clarification program at Amoral, Arkansas. We will take the $20 million from the taxpayers in Flatbroke, Florida — slowly — a penny at a time. They don't vote and they aren't paying any attention, so they won't know what hit them until it's too late."

Obviously, if you want to be financially successful, and stay that way, it is important to keep a close eye on the outcome of this diplomacy. There is money to be earned by shifting your efforts away from the folks who live in Flatbroke and toward those at Warprofits and Amoral.

It is not just Americans who are constantly courting favor with politicians to change the locations of the cones, it is also foreigners. Congress dispenses billions of dollars in foreign aid each year. There are hundreds of agents of foreign countries spending millions of dollars annually lobbying in Washington, D.C.[30]

Many in the news media like to accuse the "big corporations" and "robber baron **capitalists**" of corrupting the politicians, and some of these accusations are certainly justified. But I believe that in most cases the evidence would show these accusations have the story backward. It is the politicians who are doing the corrupting.

---

[30] "How Foreign Powers Play For Status In Washington," U.S. NEWS & WORLD REPORT, June 17, 1985, p. 35.

For instance, news stories (and school textbooks) about "robber baron" businesspersons frequently bring up the fact that during the last century it was a common practice for railroad companies to bribe lawmakers. Always omitted is the *cause* of the bribery. In THE STORY OF AMERICAN RAILROADS, Stewart H. Holbrook writes:

> Almost from the first, too, the railroads had to undergo the harassments of politicians and their catchpoles, or to pay blackmail in one way or another. The method was almost sure-fire; the politico, usually a member of a state legislature, thought up some law or regulation that would be costly or awkward to the railroads in his state. He then put this into the form of a bill, talked loudly about it, about how it must pass if the sovereign people were to be protected against the monster railroad, and then waited for some hireling of the railroad to dissuade him by a method as old as man. There is record of as many as thirty-five bills that would harass railroads being introduced at one sitting of one legislature.[31]

It would be an interesting research project to learn how many harassment bills were withdrawn versus those passed to punish firms that did not contribute enough money or other more sensuous forms of bribes.

Is this still happening? What do you think, Chris?

The FEDERAL REGISTER is the list of federal laws, and regulations, which have the force of law. In 1995, it had

---

[31] CAPITALISM, THE UNKNOWN IDEAL by Ayn Rand, Signet, New York, 1967, p. 106.

68,419 pages, up from 20,036 in 1970.[32] The regulations on businesses imposed an estimated $668 billion in costs on companies in 1995.[33] An enormous burden, one that certainly puts a lot of firms out of business.

Figuring all pages printed on both sides, 68,419 tightly stacked is 11 feet high. That's a lot of law, and it does not include the tens of thousands of pages written by state and local governments.

Are we to believe this unimaginable deluge of regulations is due to lawmakers and bureaucrats unselfishly trying to make things better? Or has the experiment with the railroads in the last century turned into a science?

In January 1996, Procter & Gamble (P&G) decided to phase out discount coupons and instead give consumers lower everyday prices. P&G had discovered that only two percent of coupons were ever redeemed and coupons ate up, each year, 6.50 billion dollars and eight million trees.

There is no law saying a company must offer coupons, but politicians went after P&G as if P&G had been guilty of some kind of atrocity. By April 1997, speeches about the consumer having a "right" to coupons had led to the New York state attorney general's office investigating P&G for "possible market manipulation."

Chris, do you think P&G was doing something crooked, or were some government officials trying to squeeze secret bribes out of P&G?

Again, Chris, if you don't get this side of the story from me you probably won't get it at all.

But I digress.

---

[32] REGULATION ORG, The Heritage Foundation, Washington, DC, 1/16/97.

[33] THE ECONOMIST, July 27, 1996, p. 19.

To prosper in a government-controlled economy, follow the dancing cones.

You said you liked the letter about clipper ships. Good. In my next letter, we're going to talk about a strategy I call the Super Clipper.

Uncle Eric

13

The Super Clipper

Dear Chris,

Up to this point I have been describing the need to follow the cones. This is the most common application of the Clipper Ship Strategy, but most people who are doing it do not realize this is what they are doing. They know nothing of cones. All they know is that they have hit pay dirt, they have stumbled onto something that works.

A variation of the Clipper Ship Strategy is more difficult to implement but even more profitable. I call it the **Super Clipper Strategy**. It was used by the real clippers of the last century.

As mentioned earlier, in the 1840s the country was in a depression. This enabled the clippers to multiply their profits. They were not only able to sell goods to the California miners at high prices, they were able to buy these goods from the *depressed* east coast where prices were down.

You can gain this same kind of **leverage** if you can find a way to follow their example. Find depressed areas — sinkholes — where people are willing to work cheap — then become the pipeline that links them with a cone.

Ideal location for a Firm

A firm should see itself as being located above the cone-sinkhole landscape. It is a plumber who runs tubing between the cones and sinkholes.

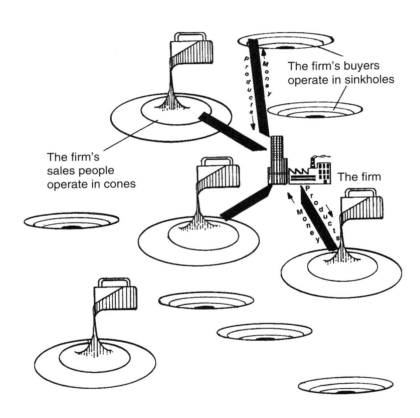

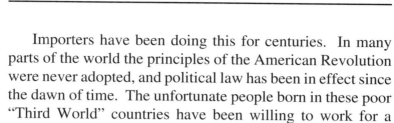

Importers have been doing this for centuries. In many parts of the world the principles of the American Revolution were never adopted, and political law has been in effect since the dawn of time. The unfortunate people born in these poor "Third World" countries have been willing to work for a pittance.

Importers may not understand the why of this sad situation, but they do understand the old principle of buy low and sell high, and they know a sinkhole when they see one. American markets have always been laden with goods marked "Made in China" or something similar.

America itself now contains many sinkholes. In 1989, after seven years of "recovery" from the 1982 recession, California's 58 counties included 14 with unemployment rates in the double digits — serious recession levels. One county had a 30% rate, that's a depression.

If you can do it, you might want to consider living in a depressed area, so that your living costs are low, and selling your products to places where people are accustomed to paying high prices. Writers have been doing this for decades. They often live in pleasant, inexpensive rural areas while selling their work to publishers who serve the large urbanized — politically active — markets.

In recent years, various kinds of cottage industries based on this principle have been springing up around the country. You may have seen TV news reports about rural families who are now earning their livings by selling their custom-crafted knitting and weaving to residents of the big cities. A movie based on this principle was called BABY BOOM with Diane Keaton.

The latest application of this principle is the much publicized wave of computer operators working in or near their rural homes far from the big cities. They use modems that enable them to phone their work into the firms that purchase their services.

Few of these people have ever heard of the cones and sinkholes or of Business Cycle Management, all they know is that they have found something that works.

Chris, in my next letter we will take a quick look at cones as they relate to the poverty problem. Until then, remember the Super Clipper Strategy, it's the most profitable.

Uncle Eric

14

Do Cones Really Exist?

Dear Chris,

"Not so fast," you say. "On the face of it, this idea of following the dancing cones sounds plausible, but a little research shows it does not make sense. Checking the latest STATISTICAL ABSTRACT OF THE UNITED STATES, I find the largest portion of the money spent by the Federal Government is to fight poverty. The so-called cones are really poor people, and if I own a business and try to establish a customer base of poor people, I will certainly go broke."

This is exactly what government officials want you to believe — they believe it, too. But the STATISTICAL ABSTRACT is a fascinating document. Turn to the section about the Federal Budget and add up all the money spent on "social spending" to fight poverty.[34] Even with a calculator, this will take a while. In his fine book FREE TO CHOOSE, economist

---

[34] A lot of money spent to fight poverty is camouflaged as something else—subsidies for schools and libraries, for instance. At bottom, the justification for the federal government to be involved in these enterprises is that some persons would not be able to afford them if these organizations had to charge full price for their services as private firms do.

Milton Friedman wrote, "There is a ragbag of well over 100 federal programs that have been enacted to help the poor."

Get your total, then go to the section about poverty. Divide the number of poor people into the amount of money spent to help them.

You will find that if all the money the Federal Government spends to fight poverty was handed directly to the poor, each family of four poor people would be receiving more than $70,000 per year. This, remember, is federal money only. Were we to add in state and local money, each family would surely be receiving more than $80,000. Tax free. Per year.

Think about it. If this were done, in the first year the family could live comfortably on $40,000 and invest the other $40,000 to set up its own business to earn a good living from then on. Poverty would be virtually eradicated in one year!

But a quick drive through the nearest inner city makes it obvious that the poor are not receiving $80,000 per year. So, if the poor aren't receiving the money, who is?

People who aren't poor.

The cones do exist and they are fat and juicy.

Incidentally, there's little chance this fraud will be abolished any time soon. Economists have been screaming about it for years, and in 1980, Thomas Sowell, a black economist who grew up in the ghetto, complained about it on national TV. But in 1979 we had finally reached the point where 50.2% of the people, a majority, were getting money from the government. If the $80,000 were given to the poor, and poverty were erased, there would no longer be an excuse to collect and redistribute money.

Americans suppose that social-welfare programs are about helping the poor. This is not true. More than 85% of all benefits go to the middle and upper classes, both old and young. Households with incomes above $100,000 get slightly more federal money each year than those earning a tenth of that.[35]

— THE ECONOMIST

This hoax would be comical if it were not so wasteful. The middle class and wealthy pay nearly all taxes and get most of the subsidies. In effect, they are subsidizing themselves. The government takes a dollar from one pocket, keeps part, and pours the change into the other pocket.

The middle class and wealthy are not only grateful for this financial "help," they vote for politicians who promise to give them more. At each election, the politician who wins is the one who can most convincingly say to the audience, "I will give you everything you want and you will not need to pay for it, the person standing next to you will pay."

Government is the great fiction, through which everybody endeavours to live at the expense of everybody else.

— Frederic Bastiat (1801-1850)
ESSAYS ON POLITICAL ECONOMY, 1872

Uncle Eric

---

[35] Quoted from THE ECONOMIST, January 11, 1997, p. 24.

15

The Biggest, Most Stable Cone

Dear Chris,

Social Security is a cone — and it is the biggest, most stable cone. We were all taught to admire this wonderful example of "social planning" — which is really just a **Ponzi scheme**[36] designed to buy the votes of older persons by using money taken from their sons and daughters. On June 29, 1982, the Commissioner of Social Security, John A. Svahn, gave a speech in which he explained the truth about the scheme:[37]

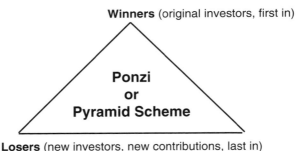

Winners (original investors, first in)

Ponzi
or
Pyramid Scheme

Losers (new investors, new contributions, last in)

---

[36] Named after swindler Charles Ponzi, a Ponzi scheme is one in which investors are paid not from income earned by the investment but from the contributions of new investors. Ponzis go broke when the number of new investors is no longer great enough to support the earlier investors. This is also called a pyramid scheme.

[37] VITAL SPEECHES OF THE DAY, September 1, 1982, p. 677.

When Social Security started it was shrouded in myth. It was sold to the Congress and the American public in 1935 as an insurance program. Each person received an account number, which implied that somewhere there was a banking type account in their name. ... As I am sure all of you know, that was just not true. ...Social Security has been the personal pork barrel of elected politicians in both houses of Congress, in administrations of both parties. ...

If you were a maximum wage earner throughout your life from when the system first began collecting taxes in 1937 and retired at age 65 in December of last year, the most — the absolute most — you could have paid into the system is $14,700. And that worker will see every penny of the $14,700[38] come back in about 19 months. And if he or she has a spouse who never worked at all, the payback will be completed within 13 months.

Now, tomorrow's worker is another study. A 20-year old average worker starting out today and paying

---

[38] This $14,700 is not adjusted for inflation. If it were, the figure would be higher but not nearly as much as many Social Security recipients seem to assume. When Social Security was first enacted, the maximum tax was only $30 per year, and in 1970 it was still only $374. Ergo, much of the $14,700 was not paid in until recently, *after* the severe inflation had already affected the dollar. Also, inflation has been severe but it certainly has not increased 100 times since the 1930s as the tax has. The inescapable fact of the matter is that Social Security is a Ponzi; the elderly have been swindled. They made the mistake of trusting government, and now their sons and daughters are paying for it. If history teaches anything it teaches that people who trust government do great harm to their children.

only the average tax over a lifetime will probably pay more than $335,000 into the system.

So, for marketing purposes, to whom would you rather try to sell your goods or services — the young worker who is seeing his income reduced by $335,000, or his parents and grandparents who are on the receiving end of this massive loss?

The loss is growing, too. Since Svahn gave that speech in 1982, Social Security taxes have risen massively. It cannot be any other way, there are not enough of you young people to carry the load.

Number of workers supporting each Social Security recipient:[39]

1940	159.1
1970	3.7
2000	3.2
2030	2.0

In other words, after you are married, you and your spouse will be automatically saddled with one dependent even before you have children.

A popularly accepted myth is that most of the elderly are living in poverty. This is ridiculous. Check your STATISTICAL ABSTRACT, the elderly are the wealthiest group in the country. (Children are the poorest.[40]) The elderly have less debt and more reliable incomes than anyone else and many of the elderly own their homes free and clear.

---

[39] THE ECONOMIST, December 14, 1996, p. 28.

[40] Report by the House Select Committee on Children, Youth and Families, released October 1, 1989.

They also pay a lot less taxes, which means they have more money to buy whatever you might be trying to sell. Says THE ECONOMIST, "A working household with an annual income of $30,000 and one child can expect to pay more than $7,000 in tax; an elderly couple will pay $690." Also, says THE ECONOMIST, "Since 1965, total federal spending on the elderly has increased from 16% of the budget to 33%."[41]

Chris, if you choose self-employment — to be in control of your own business — plan your marketing by identifying areas of the country with solid, stable economies. This means look for ones with large retirement communities.

The senior discounts offered by restaurants and movies are not for charity to help the poor, they are to draw in the age group with the largest, most stable incomes. This is an example of firms learning Business Cycle Management through trial and error.

In my next letter we will look at another type of cone I haven't explained yet. This will fill out the model even more.

Until then, remember that the biggest, most stable cone is Social Security. During your lifetime you can expect to pay a very large portion of your **earnings** into it.

Uncle Eric

P.S. Chris, I suggest you do some research on Charles Ponzi. His story is one of the most valuable financial lessons you can learn. His scheme is continually re-invented in numerous variations by governments and private individuals around the world. (For an example of how much damage Ponzi schemes can do, research what happened in Albania in 1997.) You will probably run into Ponzi schemes dozens of times in your

---

[41] THE ECONOMIST, January 23, 1997, p .23.

lifetime, so understand them well. And remember that a Ponzi's advocates may have good intentions, but this does not keep a rip-off from being a rip-off.

Next, read the following article "How Does Social Security Affect You," then I'll follow-up with a few comments.

How Does Social Security Affect You?

By studying the operation and effects of private pension plans we see how the relationship between young and old would work if government had not gotten involved.

Human beings naturally save for their retirements. The savings go into bank accounts, stocks, corporate bonds, and other assets.

These assets are the source of money used by businesses to build factories, office buildings, and other places of work.

In other words, saving creates jobs.

Part of the money the factories and such earn is used to pay wages to the workers.

Another part is used to pay the dividends, rents, and interest earned by investors.

So, by saving and investing, people automatically create both retirement income for themselves and job opportunities for their children.

It's a beautiful system. The old help lift the young into the middle class by creating good jobs for them, and the young help the old by generating dividends and interest for them to live on.

Sometimes the saving and investing is done by a private pension plan, and this works fine, too. The pension does the saving and investing, thereby providing funding for the factories and such that will produce retirement incomes and jobs.

But what does Social Security do?

It does not invest in factories or office buildings. It just takes money from one person and gives it to another. It doesn't *produce* income, it only *transfers* it.

We know from studying private pension plans that when a pension exists, a person naturally saves less on his own. In THE NEW ENGLAND ECONOMIC REVIEW, Alicia H. Munnell has written:

> Most of the studies indicate that individuals covered by pension plans save less on their own than individuals without pension plans. For example, the most recent study, based on a 1983 survey of the income and assets of over 3800 households, showed very clearly that individuals covered by pension plans reduce other forms of saving and the rate of trade-off was roughly 68 cents for each dollar of pension wealth. Most of the other studies also had results in the 60 to 70 cents per dollar range.

For example, if pension saving increases by $177 billion, this leads individuals to reduce their other saving by $120 billion.

But that's nothing to be alarmed about because the saving and investment not done by individuals is done by the pension. The factories and office buildings are created anyhow.

But what about Social Security? When people in the past saved less because they believed Social Security would be there, *the slack was not picked up by anyone.* Unlike private pensions, Social Security does not create factories and office buildings — or jobs for the young.

We do not know exactly how much saving is reduced because of Social Security, but we can be certain it erases a lot of job opportunities for the young. It's part of the reason the young find it so hard to get ahead.

In other words, when someone today spends Social Security money, he is consuming not only his children's tax money but their jobs, too.

He has been tricked into eating his children's seed corn.

Chris, you might ask, "If Social Security did not exist, what would happen to the poor who could not save for their retirements?" To answer that, we must first ask, "How many poor would there be?" It's a good research project. Using THE STATISTICAL ABSTRACT OF THE UNITED STATES, try to estimate the amount of job-creating capital the government consumes each year and the millions of good jobs destroyed by this consumption. Also look up the billions of dollars Americans contribute to private charities each year. If the millions of jobs were not destroyed, would private charities be able to handle the number of poor that would remain? In my opinion, yes, easily.

16

Accidental Cones

Dear Chris,

Most of the cones we have examined so far are deliberate. They are created directly by government agencies injecting money into the economy in specific, *planned* locations.

An example is New York hospitals. In 1968, Congress made up a law creating the Hospital Mortgage Insurance Program in the Federal Housing Administration. The purpose was to make low-interest loans to hospitals so that hospitals could more easily expand.

The program was not well known, but hospital managers in New York learned of it and took advantage of it, going on a building spree. By 1996, they had borrowed billions of dollars and put up so many new hospitals that New York had an estimated 40% more hospital beds than patients. Money earned from the patients was not enough to keep all the hospitals running.[42]

These New York hospitals were a **Deliberate Cone,** created directly and on purpose by the government's law making.

---

[42] "New York Hospitals Are Poor," by Lucette Lagnado, WALL STREET JOURNAL, November 22, 1996, p. 1.

Incidentally, the overbuilding was an example of **malin-vestment** — investment that should not have happened. But it did happen because the government's law caused it.

Another kind of cone can be called the **Accidental Cone**. This is a cone produced accidentally by the government's fiscal, **monetary** or **regulatory policies**.

Accidental Cones can be extremely profitable but also extremely dangerous if you do not know how to handle them. This will take a bit of explanation.

In a free economy, changes in the production and distribution of wealth are organized by means of the pricing mechanism — the so-called **invisible hand**[43] of Adam Smith. When there is a shortage of something, the price rises. People are spending more money for it, which means they are spending less for something else. Small **Natural Cones** and sinkholes are created.

The rising price and increased flow of money toward the shortage item create larger profits for firms supplying this item.

Firms experience reduced sales and profits when people buy less of the items the firms are supplying.

In other words, when peoples' needs or desires change and a shortage of an item occurs, some firms are helped and others are hurt. The more astute firms that are being hurt see the rising price of the shortage item and switch to supplying this item. They leave the natural sinkholes and move into the Natural Cone.

Firms that are not so astute or that cannot switch, go broke. Their assets are sold to new firms that are better prepared to

---

[43] For further explanation of the "invisible hand" see pages 77 to 87 of Richard Maybury's WHATEVER HAPPENED TO JUSTICE? published by Bluestocking Press, web site: www.BluestockingPress.com.

deal with the changed economic environment. Their employees go to work for those firms.

This process expands the supply of the shortage item, thus alleviating the shortage.

The price of the item drops back and the purchasers then have more money available to spend elsewhere. The cones and sinkholes both flatten out.

This usually happens quickly, in a few weeks or months, before either the cones or the sinkholes have a chance to grow very large.

One place where this process is most visible is the oil industry. A barrel of oil can be split into kerosene, gasoline, diesel fuel, jet fuel, and many other products. When there is a shortage of one of these products, the price rises and refineries shift to making that product in order to earn more profits. This means they make less of something else, usually something that is less in demand.

The increased profits from producing the shortage item draw more refiners to this item, and the shortage soon abates. Then refiners look for another item in short supply, and they do it all over again.

No single item experiences a huge price increase or generates an enormous profit because refiners are always switching to fill the shortages before the shortages get very big. The cones and sinkholes are kept small.

In other words, in a free economy, the cone/sinkhole landscape tends not to be very rugged. The number of high peaks and deep valleys is small because the invisible hand works to smooth them out before they get very large. The economy is mostly a rather flat plain, and the people are all gradually uplifted by the natural progress **liberty** produces.

In a free economy, the cone/sinkhole landscape tends not to be very rugged. The number of high peaks and deep valleys is small because the invisible hand works to smooth them out before they get very large. The economy is mostly a rather flat plain, and the people are all gradually uplifted by the natural progress liberty produces.

In a government-controlled economy, everything gets distorted. The government inflates the money supply, which results in extra money sloshing around. The invisible hand becomes confused by the distorted prices. The Natural Cones become bloated, cancerous. The differences between rich and poor are extreme.

You can observe this yourself. In countries where the legal systems are still somewhat scientific, not political, the people have more freedom of speech, press, and trade, so the middle classes are large. America, Switzerland, Canada, New Zealand, and Australia are examples.

In countries where the legal systems are completely political, and freedom of speech, press, and trade are severely restricted, the middle classes are small and the extremes of wealth and poverty are shocking. Examples abound in Latin America, Africa, and the former USSR.

In a government-controlled economy, everything gets distorted. The government inflates the money supply, which results in extra money sloshing around. The invisible hand becomes confused by the distorted prices.

If an item is in short supply, some of the excess money is naturally drawn toward it and the price rises much higher than it would have if the economy had been free and uninflated. The Natural Cones become bloated, cancerous.

The unnaturally high prices in the cones produce exorbitant windfall profits — politicians sometimes refer to them as "obscene" profits — for people in the cones. Huge numbers of firms and individuals are lured into these **bloated cones.**

Then when the inflation stops, the prices of the shortage items plunge. The flow of money through the cones stops and numerous firms are left high and dry. This is a depression.

My key point is that governments do not plan for these bloated, cancerous cones to develop, and they do not know where they will develop. The invisible hand decides this.

The bloated cones simply spring up as an accidental side effect of money supply expansion. When something is in short supply, or it becomes popular or fashionable, unnaturally large amounts of money are drawn to it, and it becomes a large Accidental Cone.

Accidental Cone

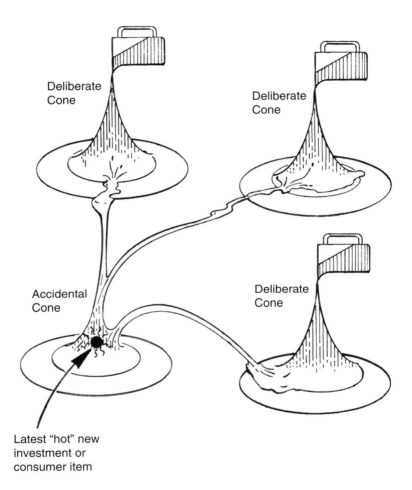

Deliberate Cone

Deliberate Cone

Accidental Cone

Deliberate Cone

Latest "hot" new investment or consumer item

After officials pour money into the economy, no one knows where the money will go. The recipients spend it wherever they wish, and this creates accidental hot spots.

In the 1920s and 1990s, the stock market became an accidental cone.

In one way or another, all firms are affected by changes in the supply and demand for money, so they all have at least a few Accidental Cone characteristics. Therefore, it is safe to assume there is no longer any such thing as a genuine, pure Natural Cone. All cones today should be classified as either Deliberate or Accidental, or **DC** (Deliberate Cone) and **AC** (Accidental Cone).

Chris, later we will get into a more complete system for cone classification, and I will explain the necessity of having a cautious attitude. If you do not know whether a cone is Deliberate (DC) or Accidental (AC), *always classify it Accidental*, it's safer. I'll be telling you why.

The need for this classification system is paramount. Many studies have been done showing that incomes in America are becoming more unequal, meaning the cone/sinkhole landscape is becoming more rugged.

This is a nationwide trend, but Business Cycle Management will help you adapt.

Until my next letter, remember that bloated cones spring up as an *accidental* side effect of money supply expansion. When something is in short supply, or it becomes the latest fad, unnaturally large amounts of money are drawn to it, and it becomes an Accidental Cone.

Uncle Eric

17

Houston: Portrait
of an Accidental Cone

Dear Chris,

During the 1970-1990 period, Houston was an Accidental Cone, one of the biggest ever.

In the 1970s, oil was in short supply, so when the government inflated the money supply, many of these new dollars went into oil. People who were flush with cash were looking for a place to put it and they began investing in oil exploration companies, oil drilling companies, oil tankers, and a lot of other oil-related enterprises.

In retaliation for U.S. backing of Israel in the 1973 Arab-Israeli war, Arab oil producers united to form an oil cartel. This **cartel** raised the price of crude exorbitantly, sucking tens of billions of the newly created dollars into the world oil markets. Every oil producing area of the world became an Accidental Cone.

Houston became one of the hottest spots on earth. Money flowed through the city like water through an aqueduct, and many **entrepreneurs** became convinced oil was headed for $50 per barrel. Some predicted $100.

A euphoric frenzy developed, and glass and steel office buildings were popping up like daisies. Jobs were so plentiful in Houston that workers from the north seemed to descend in convoys. Prosperity was Houston's middle name.

Then came the financial panic of 1979-80. People were losing confidence that the dollar would retain its value, and they began frantically trading their dollars for gold and silver.[44] As gold hit $850 per ounce and silver $50 per ounce, the Federal Reserve began to tighten.

Growth of the money supply was restricted, and the rising oil prices of the seventies became the falling oil prices of the eighties. Houston's cone began to wither and die. By 1985 the boom was dead.

Like the clipper ships, entrepreneurs who could move to greener pastures did. Those that could not, went broke.

Large buildings on concrete foundations cannot be moved, so many of the shining new office towers became high rise ghost towns. Some were offering two years rent free to attract tenants. There were 30 million square feet of unoccupied floor space — 10 million more than the total commercial footage in all of San Diego.

Chances of renting new apartments were judged so poor that developers decided to destroy them rather than maintain them empty. By 1988, five thousand apartment units per year were torn down.[45] Another dramatic example of malinvestment.

---

[44] For an explanation of velocity, read Richard Maybury's book THE MONEY MYSTERY, published by Bluestocking Press, web site: www.BluestockingPress.com.

[45] "For Texas Picture Is Gloomy," by Jeff Franks, REUTERS, June 26, 1988.

The hopes and dreams of a great many decent, honest, hard-working people were smashed, and not one in a thousand understood why. They had invested their hearts, souls, and life savings in an Accidental Cone that was only temporary.

Chris, I write these letters to you because I don't want to see you, and the family you may someday have, caught unaware in an Accidental Cone like Houston. If I could, I'd make it possible for only good things to come your way. I have no power to do that, but I can warn you about the hazards, and point out the opportunities. Throughout history there have been hundreds of giant Accidental Cones like Houston, and thousands of smaller ones, and I am sure there will be a lot more in the future.

Uncle Eric

18

Other Accidental Cones

Dear Chris,

Beware of the stock market, it has a tendency to become a bloated cone. In the 1920s the government was inflating the money supply, and the stock market had become fashionable; much of this new money flowed into stocks. The Roaring Twenties roared until the inflation stopped and the market crashed in 1929.

This was repeated in the 1980s. To bring us out of the 1982 recession, officials injected huge amounts of new dollars into the economy. Much of this new money went into the stock market, which boomed. In 1987, the injection of money was slowed and the market crashed.

If you had owned a business and your customers had been stock investors or brokers during the 1980s, they would have been feeling much more wealthy and capable of buying whatever you were selling. But you would not want to have counted on this new demand continuing. After the 1987 crash, the luxury car dealers and jewelers in the Wall Street area of New York experienced wrenching drops in sales as thousands of brokers were laid off.

Real estate was an Accidental Cone during the 1970s. Your parents might remember when almost everyone in the country was convinced real estate could only go up because "they aren't making any more of it." Fortunes were dropping into the laps of investors who knew nothing of real estate except that their brothers-in-law had told them to buy it.

If any of these investors had been your customers at that time, they would very likely have been pouring a lot of money into your pockets. But after the Federal Reserve began to tighten in 1979, many of these investors were wiped out. They had climbed to the top of the cone on the assumption the flow of money would last forever, and when the flow stopped they refused to believe it and did not bail out. They were not clippers.

A full decade after the 1979 tightening, conditions in Denver remained so bad that housing prices were down 70%[46] — yes 70%.[47]

Accidental Cones (ACs) are probably more common than Deliberate Cones (DCs), and many are larger and far more profitable. They also tend to appear faster because the market mechanisms of supply, demand, and price move faster than government agencies do. But this speed is also what makes Accidental Cones more dangerous. They can disappear overnight — witness the stock market in 1929.

The electronics industry is another example. Between mid-1982 and mid-1983, officials expanded the money supply at a 13.1% rate and a great deal of this flowed into the electronics industry. Electronics began to boom, but only until the Fed tightened again. When money supply growth dropped to 3.9% in 1984, that was the end of the electronics boom. In December of 1985, newspapers in the Silicon

---

[46] "Mile High and Down In The Dumps," THE ECONOMIST, December 3, 1988, p. 33.
[47] "A Roof But No Shelter," U.S. NEWS & WORLD REPORT, March 6, 1989, p. 45.

Valley area were running stories about the Grinch who stole Christmas. The 1983-84 Silicon Valley hot spot was one of the shortest-lived on record.

Remember, Chris, when you find an Accidental Cone, don't expect it to last very long. It might last for decades, but like the 1929 stock market, it might also turn into a sinkhole at any moment. Always be on the lookout for newer and better cones. Be a clipper.

How do you know when a cone is about to turn into a sinkhole?

Remember my letters about line functions and *the importance of watching a firm's sales.*

Pay little attention to a firm's or geographic area's production functions, watch sales. When you see sales dropping, this is a sign the flow of money may be slowing. Get cautious. Check the Federal Reserve's money supply statistics. (You can do this by subscribing to U.S. FINANCIAL DATA published by the St. Louis Federal Reserve Bank, P.O. Box 442, St. Louis, MO 63166, phone: 800-333-0810, web site: www.stls.frb.org/publications. Web sites change frequently, if you are unable to access a web address, try an Internet search.)

Has the Fed been tightening the money supply? If so, and if sales are falling, get out your list of possible new cones — firms or areas with rising sales. Batten your hatches and prepare to sail off to a more promising area. More about how to compile this list later.

This is a good spot to give you a warning. Few guidance counselors or others who help young people plan their careers know much about economics or cones and sinkholes. When they see a sector of the economy that is booming, they sometimes advise young people to get college degrees in the skills needed in these hot spots.

When I was young I had a neighbor who studied to be an aeronautical engineer. Aeronautics was booming at that time and when my neighbor got out of college he got a job with Rockwell. Then the government cut its spending on aircraft, and Rockwell went into a severe recession. My neighbor lost his job and was unable to find another because his skills were highly specialized for the aeronautics cone that had collapsed.

This is why I advise young people to acquire some generalized skills in addition to the specialized skills needed for their chosen career field.[48] A minor in business with an emphasis in marketing is a precaution that could pay off handsomely someday. Consider it a type of insurance policy.

Incidentally, Chris, if you have good selling skills, you can always earn a living. Here's why.

Essentially, a person has three economic choices. He can live as a self-sufficient hermit, producing everything he needs himself. He can use force to take what he needs. Or he can trade his production for the production of others.

Most of us choose to be traders, which means we choose to sell our goods or services.

So, there is always a need for someone who is good at bringing buyers and sellers together, a sales person.

If you are good at selling, you can always put food on the table.

Uncle Eric

---

[48] For more on the need for generalized skills, see UNCLE ERIC TALKS ABOUT PERSONAL, CAREER AND FINANCIAL SECURITY, revised edition (2004) by Richard J. Maybury, published by Bluestocking Press, web site: www.BluestockingPress.com.

In our friendly neighborhood city of St. August-
ine, great flocks of sea gulls are starving amid plenty.
Fishing is still good, but the gulls don't know how to
fish. For generations they have depended on the
shrimp fleets to toss them scraps from the nets. Now
the fleet has moved.

— Fable of the Gullible Gulls
READER'S DIGEST, October 1950

19

Hollow Cones

Dear Chris,

A cone collapses because it becomes hollow. The firms and individuals in the cone organize their plant and equipment to exploit the money flowing through the cone, and when the money stops flowing this plant and equipment become idle. With the money drained away, the plant and equipment are overhead with no purpose.

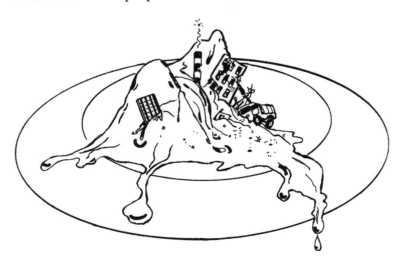

Perhaps the most cruel type of cone is the Accidental Cone stocked with plant and equipment in the *expectation* that a flow of money will soon develop. For example, in 1982 it had become apparent that Sacramento was one of the more recession resistant areas of the country, so thousands of people became convinced the area was about to boom. In 1983 the Fed's monetary policy was loosened, and office buildings began popping up in Sacramento just like in Houston.

But, in 1984, the Fed tightened again, and when Sacramento's mountainous new cone arrived, it turned out to be only a molehill. By the end of 1985 the Sacramento office vacancy rate was 25%.

In short, Sacramento's office building boom was a cone that failed to fill. Later in the decade the situation improved, but not before many good people were hurt.

Generally, **Hollow Cones** that develop in advance of a flow of money are the result of forecasts — meaning, often, puffery and propaganda. For one reason or another, someone wants you to believe an area is about to boom. Perhaps they own something in this area and they hope to sell it to you. Or perhaps they only wish more money to pour into the area so that a general increase in prices will lift the value of their holdings.

Whatever the reason, these people assemble a huge amount of data "proving" the boom is coming. The forecast is published and soon hundreds of people are pouring their life savings into the area. Ask them why and they will say "because everyone knows the area is about to boom." Sure enough, a boom begins, not because the forecast was correct, but because the forecast lured naive investors into the area.

Will the boom continue? Maybe, maybe not. These **production booms** are high risk bets. **Sales booms** — that is, booms caused by a real flow of money — are much safer.

No one can predict the future with much accuracy. Many forecasts are nonsense and are dangerously misleading, they are based on the assumption the government's behavior is predictable. But as we have seen, government officials are human and *they change their minds.* Their cone-creating policies are in a constant state of flux.

Any Deliberate Cone can dry up in a matter of months, and an Accidental Cone can vanish within days.

If you encounter one of these forecasts, question the premises. Is there a reason to believe the money supply in the area is about to increase? What *specifically* is happening to cause the boom? Has *evidence* of the new flow of money actually been *observed* — are sales really increasing — or is the demand merely being predicted?

Chris, the following illustrations may be some of the most important you will ever see. Remember them well.

Uncle Eric

A Deliberate Cone

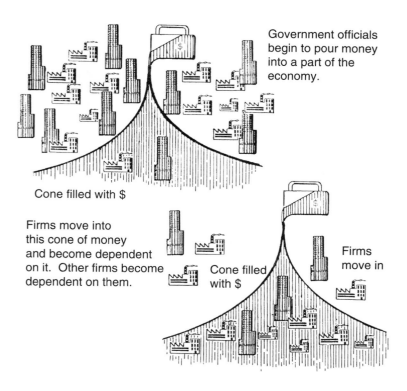

Government officials begin to pour money into a part of the economy.

Cone filled with $

Firms move into this cone of money and become dependent on it. Other firms become dependent on them.

Cone filled with $

Firms move in

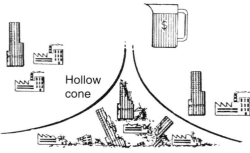

Hollow cone

Sooner or later officials then change their policies or laws. The supply of money dries up. The cone becomes a hollow structure of plant and equipment with no money flowing through it. Result: bankruptcies, unemployment, and poverty.

A Hollow Cone

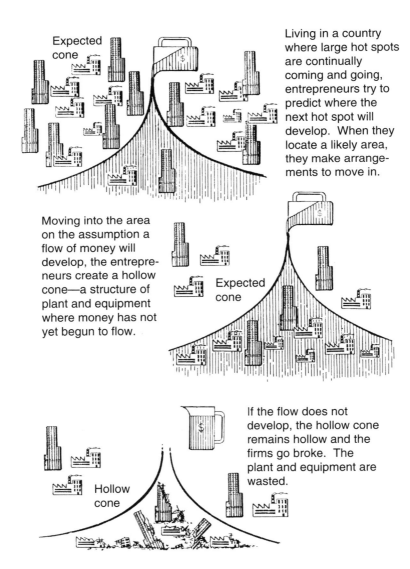

Expected cone

Living in a country where large hot spots are continually coming and going, entrepreneurs try to predict where the next hot spot will develop. When they locate a likely area, they make arrangements to move in.

Moving into the area on the assumption a flow of money will develop, the entrepreneurs create a hollow cone—a structure of plant and equipment where money has not yet begun to flow.

Expected cone

If the flow does not develop, the hollow cone remains hollow and the firms go broke. The plant and equipment are wasted.

Hollow cone

20

An Ecosystem in Chaos

Dear Chris,

Every time I look at the illustrations of the cones included in my last letter, I think of the Biosphere 2 project. Biosphere 2 is a $200 million closed ecosystem built in Oracle, AZ.

The purpose of the Biosphere experiment in the early and mid-1990s was to create a complete, sealed self-sustaining ecology that would produce all the oxygen, food, and other necessities for human life.

Biosphere 2 contained a complete, balanced array of plants, animals, minerals, and chemical elements. Huge amounts of time and energy were spent by scientific experts to make it all work.

But things kept getting out of balance. Too much nitrogen, not enough oxygen. Too many ants and cockroaches, not enough vitamin B12.

Aquatic habitats became polluted. Morning glory vines ran wild and choked out other plants.

Additional time and money were spent to force things back into balance but, in the words of professor Joel E. Cohen of Columbia University and scientist David Tilman of University of Minnesota, "Even these efforts did not suffice to keep the closed system safe for humans or viable for many non-human species."

In an article[49] about Biosphere 2, Cohen and Tilman concluded, "No one yet knows how to engineer systems that provide humans with the life-supporting services that natural ecosystems produce."

As I said in an earlier letter, the economy is an ecology. When the government intervenes beyond enforcing the two fundamental laws that make civilization possible (Do all you have agreed to do and do not encroach on other persons or their property[50]) it is playing God.

The economy is made of biological organisms — humans — and it is far too complex for any government to understand or improve. Any government action beyond enforcing the two laws creates imbalances — large, artificial cones and sinkholes that eventually result in business failures, unemployment, and poverty.

Chris, if you do not remember anything else from my letters, I hope you remember this: *an economy is not a machine, it is an ecology*, the most complex ecology in the world. The economy is comprised of millions of individuals, each of whom is so complex he has trouble understanding himself. How could anyone understand the needs, wants, and desires of millions of strangers?

Uncle Eric

---

[49] "Earth May Be The Only Safe Place," by Joel E. Cohen and David Tilman, an article from SCIENCE MAGAZINE reprinted in the SACRAMENTO BEE FORUM, November 24, 1996, p. 1.

[50] For a thorough discussion of the two fundamental laws, see Richard Maybury's book WHATEVER HAPPENED TO JUSTICE? published by Bluestocking Press, web site: www.BluestockingPress.com.

21

Outside Sales

Dear Chris,

Remember this: *Accidental Cones are the cause of recessions and depressions.* When the government restricts the money supply, these cones become hollow and collapse.

The realization that Hollow Cones exist is especially important to **outside sales** people (sales people who go to the customers rather than stay in an office where customers come to them). At one time or another you will probably work as an outside salesperson, or do similar work, so we will use it as an example. The lesson will apply in many ways throughout your life, in your career, business, and investments.

Suppose you are a business equipment salesperson working your territory. For six months you have been watching a new office building under construction. You intend to try to sell equipment to the new firms that will move in.

Finally the day arrives when the building is finished and you begin knocking on doors. On average, your company estimates a salesperson must make five calls on a prospect before a sale is made, so you are not surprised when all the new firms in the building tell you they aren't interested right now but come back in a few weeks.

You come back in a few weeks, but they still aren't ready to buy. You come back again, and again, and again. Nothing. These people seem very interested and assure you that any day now they will be ready to sign, but no matter how much you talk with them trying to meet their needs, they will not make the final commitment. Sometimes you feel they are teasing you, and you are wasting vast amounts of time and money that could be spent elsewhere. On top of this, your manager is enraged because you keep telling him you will bring in the orders any day now, and he has been waiting for weeks.

Each time you visit this building you notice most of the secretaries seem to be working crossword puzzles. The managers are reading newspapers.

It may well be that you have stumbled onto a Hollow Cone. The firms in the new building were established on the assumption there would be a strong demand for their products, but the strong demand hasn't yet materialized. These firms *appear* prosperous. You can see they have spent a fortune renting and furnishing their fancy new offices. But the truth is that they are actually in big trouble. Some politician or bureaucrat somewhere has changed his mind about something, and the cone that was beginning to develop in this area died in its infancy.

The solution to this problem is to always **qualify** your prospects on your *first* visit. "Qualify" means not only the usual process of trying to find out if they are interested and capable of buying your product, but something more. Remember the line functions of sales and production.

The prospects may honestly believe they are capable of buying because they believe demand for their product will soon be strong. So casually ask them *why* they think demand will be strong. Is it because they know a flow of money is developing — they've seen the new income stream with their own eyes — or is it because someone sold them on a *forecast* claiming the stream was coming?

If you see signs of a forecast instead of real demand, your time and energy will be better spent elsewhere. Keep an eye on these prospects — there is always the chance the forecast will make a lucky hit — but spend the bulk of your time with prospects in areas where there is a real, *observable* demand for their products. You want evidence — not wishful thinking.

Is the store or office crowded with customers? Are the customers buying or just looking?

Is the parking lot crowded? Are products being shipped from the loading dock?

I have found one of the best ways to get the necessary information is to ask the old question, "How's business?" The answer you want to hear is, "Great! Sales this month are up 8% over last month."

Answers you do not want to hear are, "Great! Production this month is up 8% over last month," or "Great! We brought in another partner and now have 8% more **capital**[51] to work with." Both these answers are about production, not sales.

In other words, if the prospect is happy to tell you about sales, then his cone is probably "filled" or filling. But if he keeps steering the conversation away from sales and toward production (or investment) then his cone may be "hollow."

---

[51] Capital is the buildings, office equipment, and other tools that workers need to produce what we want to buy—or the money saved to buy these things.

A **Filled Cone** is one that has lots of money running through it. A Hollow Cone is one with plant, equipment, and workers; but little money. You might classify Accidentals as **ACF (Accidental Cone Filled)** and **ACH (Accidental Cone Hollow).** Seek ACFs and avoid ACHs.

I stumbled onto the usefulness of this "how's business" question in 1984 when I realized Sacramento's office building boom was continuing even though I heard building owners complaining about having trouble renting offices. By the end of 1985, I realized the only developers who were doing well were those who had been happy to tell me not about the steel, concrete, and square footage in their buildings, but about the number of leases already signed.

In some cases, the forecasts on which the Sacramento projects were based were created by the developers themselves — I suppose to pull in investors — even though it was obvious the developers knew no more about economics than I know about steel and concrete.

Chris, in my next letter I will talk about the benefits of understanding cones and the Clipper Ship Strategy. Until then, remember that a lot of investment is done on the basis of wishful thinking and little else. Before getting deeply involved in a cone, look for *evidence* of real flows of money, which means look for strong *sales* to see if the cone is healthy.

Uncle Eric

22

Benefits of This Understanding

Dear Chris,

It is, of course, impossible to precisely measure the benefits of understanding cones and sinkholes and applying the Clipper Ship Strategy. But when I think of all the Hollow Cones I have spotted over the years, and the number of good people ruined by them, I can only conclude that those benefits must be enormous.

This is especially so when I observe the prosperity of persons who have stumbled onto portions of the Clipper Ship Strategy, and compare this with the plight of the millions who suffer job losses, bankruptcies, and consequent divorces, alcoholism, and who knows what else, when their cones collapse.

Chris, if you have a relative or friend you care deeply about, warn them about the cones, especially the Hollow Cones.

During the 1950s and '60s, it became policy in the schools to teach children that we will never have another depression. Supposedly, the Employment Act of 1946, the FDIC, Federal Reserve and other government agencies all insure that a depression cannot happen.

By the end of 1982, a lot of people who were taught this were living in packing crates and sleeping under bridges. The main reason I write these letters is that I care about you and don't want to see you end up like that. Most of those unfortunate people worked hard for years, but, because of their limited knowledge of economics, they were unable to protect themselves financially. By understanding economics and the Clipper Ship Strategy you should be able to achieve and maintain a comfortable, satisfying way of life.

A nationwide depression may be unlikely in any given year, but each year hundreds or thousands of cones collapse and drag down the people in them. These people suffer their own private depressions. I wonder how much drug addiction, crime, spousal abuse, and other trouble is caused by the cones.

I remember one California family who worked hard and saved their money until they could put a down payment on a house. They made payments for years, building up their **equity** until it was about $60,000. Life was going well and they were optimistic about their futures.

Then their cone collapsed. The Federal Reserve tightened its monetary policy, causing the man's employer to go out of business. Their house lost so much of its value that all of their equity, including their down payment, disappeared.

They finally gave up trying to recover in California and moved to Denver where business was booming. They bought another house and began making payments. They got their equity up to about $50,000, then the Denver cone collapsed. They were broke again.

I am sure you or your parents know people who have similar stories to tell — about good people ruined each time their cones danced away.

If you know teachers who are still telling students that depressions are impossible, you might want to pass these letters along to them. It's important that they begin to tell students that cones are always dancing off to new locations. Small, localized depressions are common. This is why you must make the Clipper Ship Strategy part of your life plan. Always be ready to follow the dancing cones.

Uncle Eric

23

Tax & Regulatory Cones

Dear Chris,

Accidental Cones can also develop from the government's tax and regulatory policies. For example, during the 1980s one of the fastest growing new fads among state governments was the creation of "enterprise zones." These were geographic areas in which firms received various tax breaks and regulatory exemptions.

Legally, an enterprise zone could be as small as a city block or as large as a whole county. State officials hoped the reduced tax and regulatory burdens would induce entrepreneurs to create new firms and more jobs in these areas.

Strictly speaking, these cones were not really accidental, officials were deliberately trying to create them. But the officials had no specific plan in mind, and the exact nature, size, and longevity of these cones was left almost completely to chance. One of the less publicized aspects of enterprise zones was that the **legislation** creating them was often only "enabling" legislation. State officials were giving local officials *permission* to establish zones.

The local officials may or may not have risen to the bait. And, if they did, they may or may not have spit it out. In other words, they could set up the zone and promise the reduced burdens, then a few years later *change their minds* and reimpose the burdens.

Checking on this in California, I found the state government enacted the enterprise zone law but did not create an enforcement mechanism to back it. Suppose a firm was created in a zone on the assumption the reduced property taxes and other regulations would enable the firm to be profitable. Then a few years later, after an election, the newly elected local officials decided to reimpose the taxes. The state would do nothing. The firm would need to hire a team of lawyers and go to court to sue the local government, and the outcome of the suit would be very uncertain.

Tax and regulatory policies also aggravated the 1980s office construction boom. Said Anthony Downs of the Brookings Institution in 1985, "Office vacancy in 31 major metropolitan areas has risen from less than 5% in 1981 to over 16% in downtowns and almost 20% in suburbs." Why? Because "for syndicators, the benefit is tax shelter, increased by the 1981 Tax Act. For savings and loans and banks, the benefit is federal deposit insurance. Since late 1982, they have offered such insurance combined with savings rates unlimited by regulations. As a result, investors have flooded these institutions with money since 1983," and these institutions poured much of this money into office construction.[52] The office glut remained a major problem until the 1990s.

Again, the economy is not a machine, it is an ecology. When governments try to improve it, they are playing God, and the results are not pretty.

---

[52] WALL STREET JOURNAL, October 29, 1985.

Summarizing, changes in taxes and regulations confuse the market's natural steering mechanism of supply, demand, and price. They help mold the cone/sinkhole landscape into mountains and chasms instead of gently rolling hills and plains.

Uncle Eric

24

Marginality

Dear Chris,

A tiny change in a tax or regulation can have an enormous effect on you due to a principle economists call **marginality**. This is the old "straw that broke the camel's back" principle. Here's what can happen.

Suppose you are the 65-year old owner of a small hamburger stand in San Diego. The stand employs a dozen young people and provides you with an income, but it is not making you rich. The difference between what you are earning now and what you could be earning if you retired and lived off your savings and Social Security is not great.

Also suppose I am an affluent resident of your area, a steady customer. At least twice each week my family eats at your stand, which means we account for about $40 of your weekly sales.

Now suppose the government has slowed the growth of the money supply recently and a recession is beginning. The recession hits some areas harder than others, and one of these hard-hit areas is on the other side of the country, Tampa.

The government wants more money to help the unemployed in Tampa, so it raises my taxes in San Diego $40 per week. I protest, but no one joins me because everyone knows affluent people can easily afford another $40 per week. All the affluent need do is stop eating out so often — a small sacrifice compared to the need to help the desperate unemployed in Tampa.

So I and dozens of other affluent people in your area stop eating out so often.

Suddenly you notice sales have fallen off a bit and your marginally satisfactory income is no longer satisfactory. You close the stand and retire. You had hoped to sell the stand, but now that its sales are declining, no one will touch it. However, this is no great loss to you, it wasn't worth much.

But your dozen employees are laid off. And other marginal restaurants around the city have closed, so unemployment and poverty are now rising in San Diego.

Three points: First, since I am affluent, the extra $40 tax has very little effect on me. "Tax the rich and give to the poor" sounds noble and justifiable because the rich really *can* afford the tax.

Second, the tax also has very little effect on you. When you retire, your standard of living will not change one iota, you will just have more time to go fishing.

Third, the people hurt most by the tax were your employees, the lowest income people in our story. These innocent, politically naive young people were two steps *downstream* from the tax increase.

Even further downstream were more firms and individuals who will be hurt because your employees who lost their jobs can no longer make as many purchases.

In short, any new tax or other change in political law, no matter how small, is a straw that will probably break some camel's back somewhere. It will create a sinkhole.

Advocates of "tax the rich" schemes might claim I am being misleading. My $40 did not disappear, it went to Tampa where it will increase spending. The loss in San Diego is offset by a gain in Tampa, they claim.

A fact always ignored in these cases is that money travels better than hamburger stands. My money went to Tampa, but your hamburger stand stayed in San Diego, empty, wasted, condemned, and eventually torn down. The total amount of job-creating capital in the country was reduced.

For the country as a whole, a net loss has occurred, and your former employees and the firms dependent on them are the people bearing the brunt of it, not me, the person who was taxed.

It is probably a fair generalization to say that for every new cone the government creates there will be one or more sinkholes that will together be of equal size to the cone. But they will probably be scattered so that the damage is not as noticeable as the cone. Legislation is usually written to achieve this effect.

Inflation is probably the most effective method of building a cone by creating thousands of little-noticed sinkholes. Print all the money that goes into the cone. Increasing the supply of dollars reduces the value of each individual dollar by only a very tiny amount, and the effect is spread across the entire population. Each person has his buying power reduced by a tiny amount.

Of course, when governments hit on this scheme, they usually decide that if it worked so well for one cone, why not use it for lots of cones, and the eventual result is **runaway inflation**.[53]

---

[53] Explained in WHATEVER HAPPENED TO PENNY CANDY? by Richard Maybury, published by Bluestocking Press, web site: www.BluestockingPress.com.

To summarize, because of this principle of marginality — the "straw that broke the camel's back" — tiny changes in taxes or regulations thousands of miles away can have severe, *unforeseeable* consequences on you or the people to whom you sell your goods or services. Sometimes you will have a cone disappear and you will never know why. Don't kid yourself into thinking it will come back. It might, but in the long run you will be better off with a policy of always being ready to shift to newer and better cones. Be a clipper.

Uncle Eric

25

Marketing Managers

Dear Chris,

Marketing managers have long known about hot and cold spots in the economy. They observe sales suddenly skyrocket in a geographic area or among a demographic group, then just as suddenly drop back. These events have been mostly regarded as random **anomalies**.

Some marketing managers are aware of Deliberate Cones, but I have yet to meet one who understands Accidentals. Understanding Accidental Cones would make their jobs easier and more profitable. Here is a mental picture you should find helpful.

Imagine the government sending a wave of bureaucrats across the country to collect five dollars from each American. The wave starts at the East Coast and moves westward. When it arrives in San Francisco all the money is loaded onto a C-130 cargo aircraft to be carried back to Washington.

But along the way the plane flies into a storm and develops engine trouble, and the crew is forced to jettison the load. They don't know exactly where the money landed, all they know is that it was somewhere over Nebraska.

But the residents of Bustedflat, Nebraska know. Money has suddenly come raining down from the sky. They don't know why, all they know is that they like it. No one has reported the loss, so the money is a literal windfall. What do they do?

What would you do if you were a merchant in Bustedflat? Knowing what you know about Accidental Cones, you would immediately raise all your prices. Your competitors would make all the early sales, but as soon as their inventory was cleaned out, the overflow demand would arrive at your store. Your profits would be greater than anyone else's.

What would you do with the profits? Would you sit on them and *wait* for more wholesale merchandise to be imported into the area so that you could buy it, and then sell it?

No, the wholesale price of this new merchandise would be very high because the wholesalers would know they could mark it up the way clothing stores in Beverly Hills mark up items for their rich customers. The difference between your cost and your selling price would be small.

You would not wait. You would immediately pour your new pile of cash into the trunk of your car and drive to a neighboring town where prices are still low. You would buy everything you could get your hands on before other cash laden cars could arrive from Bustedflat. Thus the difference between your costs and your selling prices would remain high, and the big profits would be earned by you instead of by the wholesalers in Bustedflat.

By realizing the cone is only temporary and striking while the iron is hot, you would emerge from the incident in much better shape than you would have otherwise.

In other words, by understanding the economics of cones, you would be able to recognize when one is developing, move to the top of the cone, skim the cash, then drive to an area at the fringe of the cone and trade the cash for merchandise to haul back to the top. You'd keep doing it until the cash was dispersed and the cone flattened.

Sound familiar? That's what the clippers were doing in the runs between the east coast and California. And it's what lots of entrepreneurs do all over the world every day, although most don't understand what's really happening as well as you do. They just know that there's lots of money in some places and not so much in others, and they can earn a good living connecting the two.

Notice from this example that by dumping this deluge of cash onto Bustedflat, the government did not increase the amount of *real* wealth at all. It created no new goods or services. It only caused the existing wealth to *change hands*. It reorganized the wealth and created an advantage for those who understood Accidental Cones. When the reorganization was finished and the money dispersed, the people who were in the know ended up with larger shares of the real wealth.

Now, imagine whole squadrons of C-130s jettisoning their loads and creating accidental hot spots all over the country every year. Imagine the frantic shuffling and reshuffling of the real wealth.

Imagine how much more easily you could cope with this chaos, and emerge unhurt, if you had a portable store you could constantly move from one hot spot to another.

There are not many types of portable stores. Hot dog vendors and ice cream trucks are all I can think of at the moment.

But there are many kinds of businesses that can stay in one location and sell all over the country. Any mail order business can do this. So can magazine and newsletter publishers and computer software firms. In fact, any firm that makes small, portable, high value items that are easily transported can have its production facilities in one place while making sales almost anywhere.

The Internet is making this easier every day because it reduces the cost of offering one's goods or services to persons all over the world.

Those are the types of careers or businesses you want to get into. They are comfortable ways to be a clipper. But make sure the people you work with and depend on understand the cones, sinkholes, and Clipper Ship Strategy.

Uncle Eric

26

The Automobile

Dear Chris,

It is worth remembering that the chaos and hardship produced by the dancing cones is not as severe as it could be — thanks to the automobile. While many Americans own their own homes, thereby making it difficult for them to follow the cones, they also own automobiles that enable them to commute long distances.

The story of Anaconda, Montana,[54] is instructive. Anaconda was created in the early part of the 1900s by the copper mining and smelting operation of Anaconda Minerals Company. Throughout the 1970s, the town benefited from the high copper prices caused by the Federal Reserve's easy money policy. Anaconda was an Accidental Cone.

Then in October 1979, the Fed adopted its historic tight money policy and soon copper producers were squeezed between high fixed costs[55] of production (high overhead) and falling market prices for copper. Anaconda Company was forced to cut its operation so much that 1,100 employees in

---

[54] The Anaconda story was reported in BUSINESS WEEK April 11, 1983.

[55] Fixed costs are "overhead" — utilities, taxes, insurance and other costs that cannot be easily reduced.

Anaconda were thrown out of work. This was in a town with a population of 10,000.

Lured by Social Security, 250 of the unemployed took early retirements. Another 100 moved away. But this still left the town's unemployment rate at 15% (up from 2.4% in 1970).

Some of the remaining 750 workers set up their own "mom and pop" businesses, but others started commuting to jobs in surrounding areas. A hundred workers got jobs 400 miles away in Colstrip, Montana, where a new power plant was being constructed. These workers were staying in Colstrip during the week and coming home on weekends.

In short, here were 100 people who were unemployed until they began using their automobiles to follow the dancing cones.

The story of Anaconda shows that were it not for the automobile's ability to reach out to new cones, the amount of poverty and strain on family life in this country would undoubtedly be much worse than it is. Instead of the occasional ghetto or other localized pocket of despair, we might have whole states resembling Third World countries.

Of course, even with our mobility, the stress remains great. The next time you are on the expressway during commute hours you might look around at the other cars and wonder — how many of these people are following the dancing cones? And how many of them understand what's happened to them, as you now do?

Uncle Eric

P.S. Chris, a good research project for you is to see how many additional examples of the Clipper Ship Strategy and the dancing cones you can identify in America's past history. Let me know what you find. Here are a couple to get you started.

First example: Many times in history farmers have been victims of the dancing cones. If **commodities**[56] become fashionable investments during an inflation, a lot of the newly created money will go into the pockets of farmers. Encouraged by this bonanza, many farmers will go into debt to buy more land and equipment to expand their operations. When the inflation stops, the commodity prices crash and the farmers do, too.

In the inflation of World War I, prices of farm products doubled and so did farm debt. In the 1920s, both leveled out. (Newly created dollars in the 1920s went into stocks instead of commodities.) Then in the deflation of the 1930s, prices of farm products crashed, so farmers could not pay their debts.

Now that you know about cones and sinkholes, read John Steinbeck's GRAPES OF WRATH, or watch the movie. It's the story of a farm family caught in the Great Depression who use their truck to try to find a new cone. Steinbeck probably did not understand as much economics as you now do, and his characters certainly did not, so you will need to critically read his economic commentary. But the story itself is a good one, and it is an accurate representation of what many good people suffered in the 1930s because of the dancing cones.

Second example: You might also want to research the Transcontinental Railroad built in the 1860s. This was an enormous cone that sucked huge amounts of capital into the West creating boom towns all along the tracks. Some were mining towns, others cattle towns or farm towns. Today many are ghost towns, but several have prospered. Check the histories of Abilene, Virginia City, Chicago, Bodie, and Dodge City.

---

[56] Raw materials or natural resources: iron, coal, oil, corn, wheat, copper, etc.

27

How to Follow the Cones

Dear Chris,

Each time the government injects money into the economy new hot spots are created. The injections must then continue so that these hot spots do not cool. In other words, each injection causes more malinvestment and a greater dependence on printing-press money.

Today the disorganization is everywhere. In 1950, an injection of $10 billion stopped the recession. In 1983, $100 billion was needed.[57]

To bring the unemployment rate back down to its 1989 level after the 1991 recession, a $350 billion injection was needed. We can only imagine how much it will take to stop the next recession.

So the economy is in turmoil as the injections constantly reshuffle the real wealth. The cones dance.

The successful firms of yesterday were those who sought customers with incomes that were large. The successful firms of tomorrow will be those that seek customers with incomes that are reliable.

---

[57] See Richard J. Maybury's THE MONEY MYSTERY, published by Bluestocking Press, web site: www.BluestockingPress.com.

Chris, I don't know what kind of career you will choose or what kind of business you might own, so I can only give you broad guidelines on how to identify and follow the dancing cones or how to use the Super Clipper Strategy.

Fortunately, as I mentioned in an earlier letter, we are living in an age when information is fast becoming unimaginably abundant and nearly free. With the advent of the Internet, CD-ROMs, and other computer miracles, things are changing very fast. Any specific advice I give you will likely be outdated in a month.

The government publishes mountains of useful information for identifying cones and sinkholes. One source is the National Technical Information Service, or NTIS (Department of Commerce, 5285 Port Royal Road, Springfield, VA 22161, web site: www.ntis.gov). The last time I checked, NTIS was publishing THE GEOGRAPHIC DISTRIBUTION OF FEDERAL FUNDS. Comprising fifty-one volumes, TGDOFF provides an amazingly detailed look at the locations of the Deliberate Cones. You can identify them by size, state, city, and specific program.

Of course, that may have changed, so here are suggestions for finding the data you need when you need it.

First, become friends with a good reference librarian. I am not talking about the clerk who checks out books at the library. I am talking about someone who has a lot of training in reference materials; it's a very large, complex field. When you are ready to search for cones and sinkholes on a geographic or demographic basis, make an appointment to see the librarian and ask how to find what you are looking for.

Another excellent source is a catalog of government data sources called INFORMATION USA by Matthew Lesko, published by Penguin Books. This catalog is updated periodically and shows you how to contact more than 700,000 government experts on every subject from automobile companies to zoologists. Your taxes are paying for the research these people are doing, so make use of them.

The third suggestion is, of course, to use the Internet. Often called the "information highway," the Internet can put you in touch with any number of firms and individuals who can answer any question you might have. Be sure to look for demographic data as well as economic data, since many times it is more useful. A good place to start is with the Federal Reserve Economic Data (FRED) home page, which, at the time I write this, is www.federalreserve.gov/rnd.htm. Also, explore the Census Bureau's home page: www.census.gov/.

I hope that in the near future someone will set up a Business Cycle Management web site or clipper ship web site to list all the kinds of information that are available to help people follow the dancing cones.

In my next letter I will give you an example of how data can be collected and used to analyze cones and sinkholes.

Uncle Eric

28

A Case Study: Sacramento

Dear Chris,

For decades until the 1990s, one of the most stable hot spots in the country was Sacramento, California. Being a state capital, and therefore very politically active, Sacramento had heavy concentrations of all four levels of government — federal, state, county, and city. It was not completely immune to the business cycle, but it grew constantly and never experienced the deep recessions common to other parts of the country.

Checking THE GEOGRAPHIC DISTRIBUTION OF FEDERAL FUNDS for Sacramento during the 1982 recession, we find that the Department of Agriculture (DOA) poured $500,000 into Sacramento for a "Child Care Food" program. DOA also poured in $10,000,000 for the "Food Stamp Bonus Coupon" program.

The Department of Commerce poured in $280,000 for its "Minority Business Enterprise" program and $35,000 for its "Regional Action Planning Commission."

The 1982 Department of Commerce cone for Sacramento was $3,400,000. This might sound like a rather hefty cone for one department in one city, but compare it to the Department of Defense cone for Sacramento that year: $469,000,000.

The total federal cone for Sacramento in 1982 — when the rest of the country was on the brink of ruin — was $2.6 billion.

The residents of Sacramento may not have kept track of the exact size of their cones, but local politicians frequently reminded them to stay politically active in order to keep the cones from being moved. Some of these reminders were boldly explicit. In January 1986, an air force spokesperson gave Sacramento's KFBK radio the annual accounting for his cone. "McClellan Air Force Base," he said, "poured more than a billion dollars into the Sacramento economy in 1985." He told the SACRAMENTO BEE newspaper that "some $298 million" of McClellan's payroll "was spent in the Sacramento region" and "contracts awarded to local businesses amounted to $44 million during 1985."

Once you identify a cone that you are tapping into or that you intend to tap into, be sure to check out its longevity.

By the late 1980s, Sacramento was booming but most of this boom was from private, not government, sources. The prosperity of the city had attracted so many new businesses that the percentage of government versus private drifted downward.

The stability of the Sacramento cone was being undermined because Sacramento was evolving away from a Deliberate Cone (DC) and toward an Accidental Cone (AC). More and more it resembled Houston in the 1970s.

Sacramento was a great place to get rich — until the bubble burst — which it did in the 1990s. Look at this 1985 map and you'll see why.

Sacramento

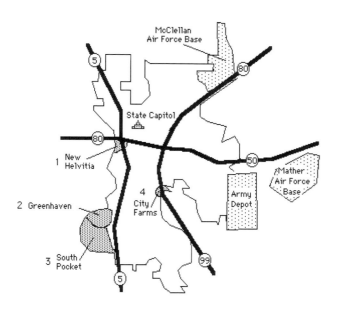

AREA	UNEMPLOYMENT RATE	PER CAPITA INCOME	MEDIAN HOME VALUE	NUMBER OF HOUSEHOLDS	EMPLOYED BY GOVERNMENT
1	35.5 %	$ 2,285	$ 52,100	649	13.0 %
2	4.9	10,340	100,700	3602	39.2
3	2.8	10,827	100,600	1708	42.7
4	20.1	4,658	27,100	487	28.0

Newspapers, magazines and newsletters derive a great deal of their income from selling advertising space, so they want their advertisers to have successful ads. To help the advertisers design the best possible ad campaigns, they gather data about their readers.

This is a small sample of the information I received free from THE SACRAMENTO BEE newspaper. The BEE's data divide the city into 73 neighborhoods, four of which are partly described here.

Sacramento had three large Deliberate Cones (DCs), Mather Air Force Base, McClellan Air Force Base, and the Sacramento Army Depot. These did a great deal to make Sacramento a hot spot. But during the Defense Department cutbacks of the 1990s, the citizens of Sacramento failed to defend these cones successfully, and Congress slashed the amount of money pouring into these cones.

The Accidental Cones (ACs), which were dependent on these DCs, were left without a flow of money. They became hollow. By 1993 you could drive around Sacramento and see empty stores and office buildings everywhere.

But the Federal Reserve was expanding the money supply, and by 1993 much of this new money was going into the stock market. Sacramento and a lot of other DC towns may have been in trouble due to the defense cutbacks, but the financial centers of San Francisco, New York, and a lot of other cities were booming. I'm sure some of Sacramento's unemployed moved to these centers and became stockbrokers participating in one of the biggest ACs ever known.

Uncle Eric

29

Hot Spots and Zips

Dear Chris,

No matter how bad general business conditions become in the country as a whole, there are always cones somewhere. Be able to locate and exploit them with great *precision*. If the country is in a recession and you aim at a cone and miss, you might hit a severely depressed area adjacent to it.

Perhaps the best way to hit a cone, especially if you are in a mail order business, is by use of Postal Service zip codes. Once you locate a likely looking cone, find its zip code and aim your marketing at that code's geographic area.

The post office sells zip code directories. Also ask your reference librarian how to contact firms that compile computerized demographic and economic data by zip code.

The digits in a zip code are organized to focus on geographic targets around the country. The first digit of a zip code indicates one of ten large national areas encompassing several states. The second indicates a state, a portion of a heavily populated state, or two or more less populated states. The third stands for a major mailing center. The fourth and fifth indicate a local mailing station.

The first three digits of Sacramento's zip are 958 and most zips on the fringes of the Sacramento cone are 956. But be careful. Be sure you hit where you are aiming. Suppose in October 1983 you had believed the government's claim that the economy was in a booming recovery, but just to be on the safe side you aimed at 958. If you had accidently hit 959 (Sierra County), you would have been trying to sell your goods or services in an area with a serious 10.2% unemployment rate. The Sacramento cone was big, but it didn't spread all the way to Sierra County.

If you had missed by a wide margin, or if you had been a bit lazy and merely aimed your marketing at California as a whole, some of your efforts may have been expended on Imperial County where unemployment was 34.2%, worse than during the Great Depression.

As late as 1989, when San Diego County was booming and had an unemployment rate of only 4.8% — one of the lowest in the U.S. — neighboring Imperial County still had 30.8% unemployment.

Uncle Eric

30

The Importance of a Model for Sorting Your Data

Dear Chris,

Economic chaos leads to a desperate search for ways to cope, which leads to a desperate search for information. Billions of labor-hours go into data accumulation and analysis. It can become an obsession.

Often, politicians are the first to acquire this obsession. No matter how much a politician believes in political power, he eventually comes to realize something is seriously wrong, the economy is a mess. Hoping to learn what kind of new laws to pass to clean up the mess, the politician seeks information.

But cleaning up a mess through the use of political power is like cleaning it up through the use of a hand grenade. The mess grows worse and the politician finds he is never able to accumulate quite enough information to know the right laws to enact. "If only I had just a little more data...," he assumes.

On top of the government's unquenchable thirst for data is the unquenchable thirst of businesses and individuals — of voters. In the United States, all this obsessive desire for information has led to enormous political pressure for govern-ment agencies to become data accumulation agencies. The Census Bureau, Labor Department, Commerce Department, and many other agencies are, to a large extent, economic intelligence services.

But there is a problem with all this data accumulation. How do you know which data are important and which are not? If, say, you read that the **Gross National Product (GNP)** is up 1.1%, is this good or bad? If you learn that industrial production has risen 2.3% and inventories 1.4%, is this good or bad? Do these statistics require some kind of response from you? If yes, exactly what is it that you are supposed to do?

The only way to separate the wheat from the chaff is to keep in your mind a picture or *model* of the way the world works. Then, when a new bit of information comes in, you know where the information fits the model — or if it fits the model.

The process is rather like that of assembling a jigsaw puzzle. How do you know where the pieces fit? You must look at the photograph of the completed puzzle on the cover of its box. This photograph is your model.

Imagine trying to assemble a puzzle that has no picture; it's just a sheet of gray cardboard. This is the situation a person is in if he does not understand business cycles and the cone/sinkhole landscape.

Without the guidance of a model, the deluge of incoming data can drive a person crazy. It can cause him to throw up his hands and walk away from the information. He tries to manage his career, business, and investments according to guesswork and hunches.

In short, the BCM model — the Clipper Ship Strategy — you've been learning from these letters, enables you to use information effectively so that your success depends not so much on your guesswork and hunches as on your skill. One way it does this is by helping you *classify* your income sources and thereby analyze the reliability of the demand for your goods and services. I've already introduced you to the simple terms DC (Deliberate Cone) and AC (Accidental Cone). To these we added ACH (**Accidental Cone Hollow**) and ACF (**Accidental Cone Filled**). I'll give you more shortly.

As for the GNP, production and inventory statistics mentioned above, our cone/sinkhole model tells us these data are too broad to be of much use. They do not focus on the individual cones and sinkholes that are important to us, so we mostly just ignore them.

Chris, the big challenge is not so much in finding data to use, but in deciding which data *not* to use. There is so much of it. BCM, or the Clipper Ship Strategy, provides the model for selecting and processing the correct data.

Uncle Eric

31

Cone Classification

Dear Chris,

For thousands of years, entrepreneurs have known how to make sales. The formula is simple:

1. Find out exactly who the customers are.
2. Find out *exactly* what they want.
3. Find a way to acquire or produce it.
4. Tell them you can supply it to them.
5. Remind them of the benefits to them.
6. Ask for the money.

Not so simple is *applying* the formula. Numbers 4 , 5, and 6 can be easy, but in today's economy numbers 1, 2, and 3 can be quite difficult. The cones and sinkholes create such obstacles that enormous amounts of time, energy, and money are often wasted. Sometimes conditions are so chaotic, a firm begins to overemphasize the three tasks it can do well, numbers 4, 5, and 6, and its sales people begin to feel like galley slaves.

To avoid this situation, deal systematically with your business environment. Gather the data necessary to classify your cones, then tailor your marketing to the special characteristics of each classification.

Before gathering your data, first decide how much *accuracy* you will need.

Uncle Eric

Sensitivity To Business Cycles*

Your customers' incomes are your income. Some industries are very cyclical, they swing wildly between boom and bust; others are very stable. Persons from stable industries should form the bulk of your customer base so that your income remains reliable. Customers from highly cyclical industries can be wonderful sources of income when they are in a boom, but the booms do not last; sell to them only on a hit-and-run basis. These cyclicality estimates are for *established* firms — those in business five years or more.

Industry	Examples	Cyclicality
Government	Public schools, police, highways, social services, libraries, military	Almost none
Durable goods	Automobiles, TVs, power tools, washers, computers, lawn mowers	High
Non-durables	Food, clothing, soap, paper, disposable diapers, gasoline	Low
Habit forming	Liquor, tobacco, gambling	Low
Capital goods	Lathes, presses, pumps, furnaces, drilling equipment, refineries,	High
Construction	Homes, offices, stores	High
Services	Beauty shops, laundry, auto repair, plumbers	Medium
Medical	Dentists, doctors, hospitals	Low
Raw materials	Lumber, iron ore, copper, gravel	High
Trade	Retail and wholesale	Medium

*Generalizations for the country as a whole.

32

Is Pinpoint Accuracy Necessary?

Dear Chris,

Earlier I referred to various states, counties, and cities as cones. I said, for instance, that Sacramento was a cone.

Bear in mind that money does not really flow into geographic areas, it flows into the cash registers, pockets, and wallets of specific firms and individuals.

Suppose you own a business. Ideally you want to be able to do your classification so precisely that you are working with specific firms and individuals. You would classify them according to their specific sources of income. The data are available to do this and the direct marketing industry uses it.

Such precision is highly effective, but it may not be worth the cost. You may do just as well classifying firms and individuals broadly, not according to their specific income streams, but only according to the industry or geographic areas in which they are located.

Examples:

If your firm is the type that sells high value goods or services to a small number of repeat customers, then you may want to get a credit bureau report on each customer.

This will cost in the neighborhood of ten dollars per customer, but it may be worth it. If, say, you are running a mainframe computer dealership or a Mercedes Benz repair shop, a single customer might account for a percent or more of your sales; you would want every customer described with great accuracy. You may want their specific incomes, debts, occupations, ages, and everything else a computerized credit report search could provide.

But if you sell less expensive items to a large number of occasional or one-time customers — if you have, say, a small computer shop or used-car dealership — then you will probably find it more cost effective to work only on the broader level of industry or geographic classification. All you may need to know is the customer's occupation or address. The reduced precision will be offset by the fact that you are aiming at a larger audience and you do not need to achieve pinpoint accuracy, you only need to be in the ball park.

Incidentally, Chris, if you are someone's employee, then you, personally, are a firm with one customer. Your employer is your customer.[58]

I suggest you go to great lengths to learn everything you possibly can about this customer. Is this customer a Deliberate Cone or an Accidental? Filled or Hollow?

Why is this important? If your customer, your employer, is a Hollow Cone, what do you think this does for the stability of your job as an employee? Think about it.

Uncle Eric

---

[58] Uncle Eric discusses this concept with Chris in more detail in the book UNCLE ERIC TALKS ABOUT PERSONAL, CAREER AND FINANCIAL SECURITY, revised edition (2004) by Richard J. Maybury, published by Bluestocking Press, web site: www.BluestockingPress.com.

33

How to Classify Cones

Dear Chris,

For each person or firm you are trying to classify, ask:
1) Is this person or firm a Deliberate Cone (DC) or an Accidental Cone (AC)?
2) Are they Filled (F) or Hollow (H)?
A Deliberate Cone (DC) is a good customer, he has a more reliable income than an Accidental Cone Filled (ACF). The ACF may have more money for the moment, but don't count on the ACF for the long run. View him as a hit-and-run opportunity. Remember Houston.

An Accidental Cone Hollow (ACH) may also be a good hit-and-run opportunity, but the ACH is in a precarious position. Don't spend much time on him, he's living off his savings, not his income.

If you'd like more precision, I suggest the use of a letter-and-number system that classifies in descending order of stability. The following is a system that should work for any firm, but each businessperson may want to modify or simplify it for his or her own use. It is far more precise than most people will ever need.

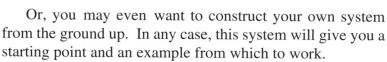

Or, you may even want to construct your own system from the ground up. In any case, this system will give you a starting point and an example from which to work.

You will notice that nearly every person you know fits into one of these categories. It might be a good exercise to list and categorize them, the skill will come in very handy later in life, especially if you have your own business or are in marketing.

Chris, dog-ear these pages so you can easily turn back to them for future reference, you will probably need to do that often.

DCF1 A Deliberate Cone, Federally created and *first (1st) in line* at the federal spigot (which is backed by the federal printing press.) These are people who have extremely steady, reliable incomes. Examples are retirees receiving Social Security, military pensioners, and civil service pensioners. These people vote and they have a great deal of political clout. Chances of their cones going dry are virtually nil. If you had a business and your firm's customers were all DCF1s, you could safely plan five or ten years into the future. Luck would play a very small part in your sales, and your success would be almost totally dependent on your skills. DCF1s are the highest quality cones, and if there is any way for you to build them into your customer base, you should expend great efforts to do so. Their stability will make life much easier for you.

DCS1 A Deliberate Cone, State created and first (1st) in line at the state spigot. Examples would be state pensioners. Their incomes are stable and reliable, but because state governments cannot print money, they are not quite as reliable as DCF1s. Still, they are high quality, get them if you can.

DCL1 A _D_eliberate _C_one, _L_ocally (city or county) created and first (_1_st) in line at the local spigot. City and county pensioners. Not as good as state or federal, but some of the best.

DCF2 A _D_eliberate _C_one, _F_ederally created and second (_2_nd) in line at the federal spigot. Examples are federal agencies or employees. These are very good cones because their incomes are straight from the federal spigot and backed by the printing press. However, these people occasionally experience the budget cuts, layoffs, and career changes that have little affect on DC1s, so they are not as stable or reliable as DC1s.

DCS2 A _D_eliberate _C_one, _S_tate created and second (_2_nd) in line at the state spigot. State agencies or employees.

DCL2 A _D_eliberate _C_one, _l_ocal agencies or employees and second (_2_nd) in line at the state or local spigot.

DCF3 A _D_eliberate _C_one, _F_ederally created and third (_3_rd) in line at the federal spigot. This is a firm or individual who earns his living selling directly to DCF1s and DCF2s. Examples would be military contractors, retailers located just outside the gates of military bases, and group insurance companies selling policies to federal employees. DCF3s can be valuable customers because their incomes do not fluctuate with the business cycle, but do not grow too dependent on them. They can be affected by federal budget cuts and layoffs.

DCS3 A Deliberate Cone, State created and third (3rd) in line at the state spigot. This is a firm or individual who earns his income by selling directly to DCS1s and DCS2s. These people can also be valuable customers because their incomes do not fluctuate with the business cycle, but they are further from the printing press than DCF3s and are also vulnerable to budget cuts and layoffs. Much of the Sacramento economy in the 1980s was DCS3s.

DCL3 A firm or individual who earns his income by selling directly to DCL1s and DCL2s. Even further from the printing press, and so even less stable and reliable, but still resistant to the business cycle.

All Deliberate Cones are resistant to business cycles. They are not immortal, but they are a lot tougher than Accidental Cones.

ACF An Accidental Cone Filled. Examples would be Houston during the 1970s, farmers during the 1970s, and stockbrokers in the 1990s. If your customers are mostly ACFs, then you should consider gathering more DCs. You are seriously in need of more stability.

ACH An Accidental Cone Hollow. Examples would be Houston and farmers in the 1980s. If your customers are ACHs, you are in big trouble. Launch a crash program to pull in DCs. If you have trouble getting DCs, then accept ACFs as an emergency measure while you continue working on DCs. Your situation is critical.

S   A Sinkhole. Examples would be slums and other poverty stricken areas, including some of the worst-case Third World countries. These are not areas to sell to, they are areas to buy from. Surprisingly, however, if you have been selling into an S for quite some time and you are still in business, your situation is probably not as critical as that of an ACH. You have somehow adapted to your environment, and your need to acquire DCs is not so desperate.

Chris, as I said, this system is far more elaborate than most people will ever need. I believe nearly everyone can get along very nicely with a mental system of just four categories: DC, ACF, ACH, and S. During the next six months or so, as you walk around town frequenting businesses and talking with people, get in the habit of mentally noting if they appear to be DC, ACF, ACH, or S, just as you might note their hair color or occupation. Once you have the habit, your economic environment will be much clearer to you, dangers and opportunities will be much easier to identify.

These four labels will also help in your study and understanding of history. The clippers sailed to San Francisco because California was a huge ACF. When the money (gold) became difficult to dig up, the clippers diverted to the new ACF, Australia.

The stock market of the 1920s was an ACF. By 1931, it was an ACH.

The great Transcontinental Railroad of the 1860s was a DC.

When Columbus came to America he was looking for an ACF. So were the conquistadors.

Hitler became popular among Germans in the 1920s and '30s because, thanks to the governments of Britain and France, Germany was littered with ACHs and Ss. Chris, if you research how the Germans were affected by Article 231 of the Treaty of Versailles, you will understand World War II as few others do.

If you ever own a business, one of the most important points you will read in this set of letters is this: *Your DCs are your source of stability and your ACFs are your source of large profits.*

When the money supply is expanding rapidly (or money demand falling) large amounts of cash are sloshing around in the economy and ACFs are growing like weeds. Be aggressive. Get out there and take advantage of these ACFs.

But remember, an ACF *is* accidental and its lifespan may be short. Never become dependent on it. When an economic downturn threatens — when money supply expansion has slowed and interest rates are rising — get ready to go back to selling mostly to your DCs. If you are not prepared to do this, you will become an ACH.

Again, DCs are resistant to changes in the Federal Reserve's monetary policy and ACs are not. The ACs often contain more money, but they are more dangerous.

Uncle Eric

34

Precision and Size of Firm

Dear Chris,

As mentioned earlier, if you do eventually own a business, the amount of classification precision you need will depend very much on the size and type of your firm.

A small firm with very few customers requires greater precision than a large firm. If you own, say, a barber shop in Sacramento, then you will want to learn a great deal about each customer — they do not all work for the government. If a large percentage happens to work for, say, one of the area's few steel mills, your business will be less cyclical if you retarget your marketing to pull in more DCs.

You will not find it difficult to gather this information. When the customer is sitting in the chair, ask him what he does for a living. Most people love to talk about their jobs, even if they hate their jobs; they will tell you far more than you will ever need to know about them.

On the opposite side of the scale from the barber shop, suppose you are the marketing manager of a major auto manufacturing company. In this case, you may find it adequate to work only on a broad basis.

For instance, every resident of Eureka, California, could be painted "probably ACF or lower." When the economy is stagnant, you can confine your marketing to "DCL3 or higher" communities, and when the economy is expanding, add the "ACF or lower" communities.

Here is a crucially important point. *If you encounter a cone difficult to classify, and the expense of accumulating the additional data needed to classify it is great, always err on the side of caution.* If you do not know whether the cone is a DC or an AC, assume AC; whether Filled or Hollow, assume Hollow.

This will keep you from becoming dependent on cones that are less stable than they appear. You will avoid a false sense of security and be better able to prepare for a sudden drop in your income.

A corollary to this is that if you own a firm but do not want to go to the trouble and expense of classifying your customers, then assume they are all ACs and set up your plant and equipment according to the instructions I'll provide shortly. This will keep you from becoming an ACH.

Uncle Eric

35

Split Cones

Dear Chris,

The effects of the 1982 recession were reduced for many firms and universities because large portions of their incomes consisted of Pentagon research money. RCA held Pentagon research contracts valued at $995,947,000; Texas Instruments, $838,977,000; Stanford University, $22,783,000; University of California, $35,345,000.[59]

But each of these firms and universities also had other sources of income that were not tapped into the government. To stay on the safe side, I would either classify them as ACs, Accidental Cones, or I would create a special category for **Split Cones — SC** — which would fall between the DCs and ACs.

As the computer revolution progresses, difficulties in classification will gradually disappear. The costs of data processing will decline to the point that it will be possible for any firm, large or small, to quickly and easily describe, label, and contact every firm or individual in the country. The only people who will remain at the mercy of business cycles will be those who do not understand them.

---

[59] U.S. NEWS & WORLD REPORT, April 4, 1983, p. 46.

After reading these letters, Chris, you should not be one of them.

Another way to classify cones is according to their sensitivity to the business cycle. A customer who derives his income from an electric utility company will have a more stable and reliable income than one who derives his income from auto manufacturing. The former is so stable it is almost as good as a DC, and the latter is one of the most unstable ACFs. You may want to note these differences when doing your classification.

It's not hard to figure out. Essentially, a cone's sensitivity to the business cycle is based on the purchasing behavior of the cone's customers. A DC, for instance — a government spending program — is insensitive to the business cycle because its money rolls in steadily despite the condition of the economy. The government's customers, the taxpayers, have no choice about purchasing the government's goods or services. If they don't pay, they go to jail.

Similarly, the most stable of the ACFs (Accidental Cone Filled) are the industries producing goods or services for which the customer cannot easily postpone purchases — food stores, water and electric companies, trash collection companies, and phone companies.

Far more sensitive to the business cycle are industries producing goods or services for which purchases can be postponed indefinitely. Auto manufacturing, for instance. If necessary, a consumer can drive his old car for many more years. The consumer can also continue living in an apartment rather than buying a house, so housing construction is very business cycle sensitive. So is swimming pool construction.

Interest rates are another important factor. When money is tight and rates are high, the makers of big-ticket items purchased with borrowed money are hard hit. Manufacturers of refrigerators, washers, dryers, and stoves are examples.

Less affected are makers of small-ticket items commonly purchased with coins and small bills. I know the owner of a large chain of corner convenience stores. He derives the bulk of his profits from sales of cigarettes, beer, and wine. Selection of locations for these stores is done very carefully, and the owner tells me sales are virtually immune to the business cycle. Even in the 1982 recession, the chain's income changed very little. People are not as careful when spending dimes and quarters as they are when spending $100 bills.

Importers and exporters tend to be very business cycle sensitive. American products are priced in terms of dollars — not francs, pounds, or other foreign currencies. To buy and sell American products, foreigners must first exchange their currencies for dollars. So, as the value of the dollar rises on international currency markets, more units of a given foreign currency are needed to purchase American products; the sales of exporters decline and the sales of importers rise because the importer can use his highly valuable dollars to buy foreign goods at bargain prices. Conversely, as the value of the dollar falls, the sales of exporters increase, but those of importers decline.

If you own a business, you might want to classify customers who are exporters as **ACE (Accidental Cone Exporter)** and importers as **ACI (Accidental Cone Importer)**, then keep a close eye on the foreign exchange value of the dollar. When the dollar is strong, you can earn more money selling your goods or services to importers. When it is weak, sell to exporters.

One way to learn the business cycle sensitivity of a customer is to ask him. In the barber shop example, ask the customer if his job or business was affected by the 1982 and 1991 recessions. Then ask him about the late 1980s and mid-1990s when the economy was doing better. After he leaves your shop, jot down his name and a few notes on a 3x5 card. Is he an **I (business cycle Insensitive)**, an **Sw (Somewhat business cycle sensitive)** or **V (Very business cycle sensitive)**?

Sort your cards into the three stacks, I, Sw, and V. Comparing the size of the stacks will give you an extremely clear picture of your customer base and your firm's sensitivity to business cycles. If you have a lot of Is, great. A lot of Vs, not great; do some advertising around government buildings to pull in DCs.

I see no reason why this technique cannot be used by other firms, too. Travel agents, dentists, veterinarians, lawyers, podiatrists — anyone who has the customer in his presence long enough to strike up a conversation.

If you don't have that kind of business, you will probably need to get computerized data on demographic and economic profiles of the zip codes where your customers live. Mountains of this data are available now, and there is a lot more coming. Ask your friend, the reference librarian. Check the Internet.

All over the country, people who know little about economics are slowly, painstakingly discovering Business Cycle Management through trial and error. Birmingham was hard hit by the 1982 recession because its economy was based heavily on steel and other industries sensitive to business cycles. But by 1989 NEWSWEEK had named Birmingham one of the "Ten Hottest Cities" in the U.S.

Through tax breaks and other incentives, Birmingham's mayor and other activists had changed the city's mix of industries. In a 1989 letter from the Birmingham Chamber of Commerce, I was told that "The Birmingham economy has become very diversified from its once dominant steel industry into other areas such as health care, engineering, and telecommunications."

I am sure Birmingham's economy will never be as stable as we would like it to be — only Washington, D.C. is that stable — but Birmingham certainly did show the benefit of applying the principles of Business Cycle Management, even though they probably know little about cones and sinkholes.

Doing research for this series of letters, I bought data from the Labor Department showing employment in various industries in the U.S. and in my state and local area going back years. I divided employment data into 100 categories of industries and checked employment stability in each category during the previous 15 years, especially in the previous recession. I found that the statistics agreed with the Business Cycle Management model.

For instance, sellers of non-durable goods such as paper and groceries suffered less unemployment than those of durable goods such as cars and refrigerators. Government had the least unemployment of all.

You could do the same for your state and local area, and select the most stable industries as the best customers for your goods or services.

Uncle Eric

36

An Eerie Feeling

Dear Chris,

Over the years I've noticed my clients who learn about Business Cycle Management fall into the habit of mentally classifying firms and individuals around them. I do it. When I first meet someone, a simple "Deliberate Cone or Accidental Cone?" question pops into my head. This will probably happen to you, too, and as you get more comfortable thinking along these lines, the system will become more detailed. Is the person an AC, and if so, an ACF or ACH?

If your experience is typical, the result will be fascinating. After you have known someone for five minutes you may know more about his future than he does. It's an eerie feeling.

I run into this most often in regard to Hollow Cones. A case that sticks in my mind was that of a small building contractor in my town who, in 1981, sunk all his capital into two $400,000 houses. At that time, the Federal Reserve's money supply statistics and interest rates were signaling the recession. Interest rates were high, the dollar was strengthening and commodity prices were heading south.

Taking a walk one day, I chanced to meet the builder and he proudly asked what I thought of his new project, which was half complete. I said I thought it was grand and he would probably make a sizable profit if he finished it fast and sold quickly. He said he wasn't worried, "everyone says real estate can only go up."

I agreed everyone was saying that, and I expressed the humble opinion that they were whistling in the dark. I was trying to make him see that the good times were about to end, but the whistling would enable him to sell at a good price if he hurried. He was clearly an ACH.

Of course, the builder didn't know me, I was just a passer-by, and he naturally assumed my advice was worth what he paid for it.

In 1986, the houses were still vacant and the builder was bankrupt.

Chris, by learning this classification system early, when you have nothing to risk, you can test your abilities to classify accurately, over and over again, until you can do it as naturally as breathing. When you are ready to start a career or business, or make investments, you will be light years ahead of most college graduates and new business owners.

The key to success is to be a clipper and follow the dancing cones, and to do that you must be able to identify cones.

Uncle Eric

37

Gathering More Information

Dear Chris,

Know thy cones! As mentioned earlier, the easiest and most reliable way to get the information necessary to classify a customer is to strike up a conversation with him. Ask him about his job.

Another easy way is through a credit bureau check, but this can be expensive for firms with hundreds of small-ticket customers.

Many firms are able to go straight to their own files to get free information. Dentists, lawyers, accountants, architects, chiropractors, and many others do not collect from the customer at the moment of the sale, they use a billing system. The billing system requires each customer to fill out a form. The form asks for the kind of information that can be used for cone classification.

If your firm is the type that cannot use a billing system — a doughnut shop, for instance — then you need to find other ways to get the necessary data to accurately classify your customers. You might put up a sign in the shop: *"Win a Dozen Doughnuts Free!"* The sign explains, "Business Card Drawing. Drop your business card in the jar. Each week we draw a card and the winner gets a free box of doughnuts." The business cards tell you the occupations.

You could also have "special weeks." One week you could put up a sign saying *"County Employees Week! One Free Doughnut to County Employees! Win a Dozen Doughnuts Free!"* The sign explains, *"Get your free doughnut by filling out the slip with your name, address, and county I.D. number, and drop it in the box. At the end of the week we draw five names; each winner receives a dozen free doughnuts."*

Next week have *"Public School Teachers Week,"* then the week after, *"State Employees Week,"* *"Auto Salesmen's Week,"* *"Construction Workers Week,"* and so forth.

Put all the names and addresses in your computer and classify them. During recessions, send ads and coupons to your DCs. During expansions, hire a few more employees and send ads and coupons to both DCs and ACFs.

A similar method for gathering information to classify cones is to advertise in publications aimed at specific groups. Run ads offering discount coupons. For instance, in a public employee union newsletter or magazine, you could run an ad: *"$2.00 Discount on Doughnuts! Send us a self-addressed-stamped-envelope and we will send you a coupon worth $2.00 on any purchase of $5.00 or more at Joe's Doughnut Shop."* The cost of the ad might be covered by renting the resulting list of DCs to other firms. You may even earn a profit from the rental.

Carrying the idea a step further, assemble a direct-mail booklet of coupons for a large number of non-competing firms. For instance, in a group marketing effort, the butcher, baker, and candlestickmaker could all pool their lists of DCs. When monetary policy is loosened and the economy is booming, they could expand the promotion to include their ACFs.

If all else fails, print up colored coupons and flyers: red for federal workers, blue for state, yellow for county, green for city. Hire people to hand out the flyers near the doors of the appropriate government office buildings when workers arrive for work.

Uncle Eric

38

Specialized Organizations and Publications

Dear Chris,

There are thousands of associations, newsletters, magazines, and other organizations and publications aimed at specific groups. As computers continue to reduce the costs of publishing, the number of these specialized organizations and publications increases, which is boon for Business Cycle Management.

Rent their mailing lists. Buy their directories. Advertise in their publications.

To find these organizations, check the Yellow Pages under "Associations." When I checked, the Sacramento phone book had 280 listings under this heading and referred to "see also:" Business & Trade Organizations, Senior Citizens Organizations, Labor Organizations, Veterans and Military Organizations, and many more. Each group can be classified as DC, AC, or ACF, and probably in a few cases, ACH and S.

Ask your reference librarian to help you locate specialized directories of associations and newsletters.

A few examples illustrating the range and specificity of associations are: the Commissioned Officers Association of the United States Public Health Service (DCF2s), the National District Attorneys Association (DCL2s), the Association of Government Accountants (DC2s), the National Association of County Agricultural Agents (DCL2s), the Building Officials and Code Administrators International (DCL2s), and the Council of Jewish Organizations in Civil Service (DCF2s).

On the local level in California, I found the California Association of Community Colleges (DCS2s), the Marshals Association of California (DCS2s), the California State Firemen's Association (DCL2s), and others.

Specialty publications I have seen over the years have included: HIGHWAY PATROLMAN magazine, FEDERAL MANAGER NEWSLETTER, THE SENTINEL newspaper for reserve military officers (a DCF1 source!), the CALIFORNIA NURSE newspaper, the CALIFORNIA STATE EMPLOYEE newspaper, and many more.

The Sacramento Chamber of Commerce provided me with its DIRECTORY OF CLUBS, ORGANIZATIONS, AND ASSOCIATIONS. This directory contains the names, addresses, phone numbers, and contact persons for some 450 organizations in the immediate Sacramento area.

To summarize, Chris, no matter what group you are trying to reach, someone else is already reaching them. No need to reinvent the wheel. To build your carefully classified customer base, go to the reference section of a large library and browse through the directories. You'll be amazed. Rent the lists, advertise in the publications, speak at their meetings.

Uncle Eric

39

External Information
A D.E.W. Line

Dear Chris,

I've heard your parents talk about the 1950s — when Americans were afraid Soviet bombers would come over the North Pole to bomb America. Your parents remember bomb drills at school, similar to fire drills today.

The government spent millions constructing parallel lines of radar stations running east to west across Canada. The most distant of these lines, and the one capable of providing the earliest warning of the coming doomsday, was the **Distant Early Warning Line**, or **D.E.W. Line** in the far north of Canada.

To keep track of the health and location of your cones, you need to surround them with your own Distant Early Warning Line of information sources. This way, anything that affects your cones will be detected before it can harm you.

Your D.E.W. Line will be easy to construct because you are not the only person who is interested in the health and location of your cones. The people in the cones are even more interested than you are, and they are constantly gathering information about it. This may be the most important reason why many specialized associations and organizations exist. They are watchdogs for their cones. They've probably never heard about the idea of cones — they are simply trying to safeguard their livelihoods.

Subscribe to their newsletters and magazines. They will tell you very quickly if there is a development affecting their cones.

This brings up an important side point. If you cannot find a newsletter or organization associated with a Deliberate Cone, this could be a sign the DC is not too healthy. The size and longevity of a DC depends ultimately on the political clout of the people in the DC. If you see no signs of lobbying or campaigning, this could mean the people in the DC have become complacent and unwilling to defend their cone.

During the 1960s, when missile contracts began running out and weapons makers failed to do enough politicking to garner support for more, employment at Sacramento's Aerojet General Corporation plunged from 20,000 to 2,000. In the 1980s it was still only 3,000.

Then the defense cutbacks of the 1990s brought even more cuts. The giant Sacramento cone collapsed because the people in Sacramento were not politically active enough to defend it successfully. Today the dollars that would have gone into Sacramento's defense industry are flowing elsewhere, probably to a place where the recipients exercise more political clout.

Let me clear up a possible misunderstanding before it arises. To be successful in a government-controlled economy, you need to sell your goods or services to people who have strong, healthy cones, and who are actively defending these cones by using the political process. This does not mean I think these people are demonstrating that political power is a good thing. I am only telling you what the reality is — and what you need to do to adapt to it to protect yourself.

The cones, and the associations, special interest groups, and lobby groups formed to defend them, are grotesque. A cone is a pile of malinvestment. It is plant and equipment that exists in a location only because political forces have lured it to that location.

If the political forces did not exist, the plant and equipment would be elsewhere. It would be serving people who have better things to do with their time than hang around the lobbies of government buildings trying to secure the votes of lawmakers. This, incidentally, is the origin of the term **lobbyist**, a person who hangs around the legislature lobby hoping for a chance to score points with a politician.

Again, as I said in my first letter, if you don't hear the non-statist side of the story from me, you probably won't hear it. All the dominant political viewpoints in the U.S. today are statist. They think political power is a good thing.

Since political law is the single greatest influence on any cone, private legislative analysts commonly publish reports and newsletters announcing and analyzing proposed laws. Many chambers of commerce have become little more than lobbying groups for business, so the chamber managers are likely to know about any newsletters you might find useful. Also, in some states, government analysts publish these kinds of reports as a "public service." Call the office of your state representative.

The FEDERAL REGISTER contains the bulk of the new Federal laws and regulations enacted each day. You will go crazy trying to read the whole thing — but you don't need to.

Recently, FEDERAL BUSINESS OPPORTUNITIES (www.fedbizopps.gov) was designated in the FEDERAL ACQUISITION REGULATION (FAR) as the single point of universal electronic public access on the Internet to governmentwide Federal procurement opportunities that exceed $25,000—in other words, a listing on the Internet announcing the creation of new cones.

Of course, we have been talking here only about Deliberate Cones, which are not too likely to dance away on short notice. For Accidental Cones, you need faster, more detailed information. It's available.

Many ACs either contain, or are associated with, companies large enough to have their stocks traded on the stock exchanges. This means there are thousands of stockbrokers and mutual fund managers constantly analyzing the health of these companies and, by extension, the health of the cones. Here's how it works.

Wall Street is a huge data processing machine. It sifts and reacts to incoming information and adjusts prices accordingly. The price of a stock reacts almost *instantaneously* to any important developments.

However, the result of the developments usually takes weeks or months to filter down to Main Street where you are operating. So the prices of the stocks are a D.E.W. Line for the cone.

This D.E.W. Line is not infallible, but there are not many human inventions that work better. If the price of a stock associated with one of your cones makes a sudden move upward or downward, you can bet something important has appeared on *your* horizon. Call your stock broker and find out what it is.

Speaking of infallibility, let me emphasize that Business Cycle Management or, if you prefer, the Clipper Ship Strategy, is by no means perfect or even complete. Economics is a young science and we have much to learn. It is, after all, the study of humans, and humans are the most complex creatures on this planet. Any one of them is a mystery, even to himself. Millions together are probably so complex we may not have a good working model for thousands of years.

But, until we get that model, we need to use something to help us get through our everyday lives, and I've found the BCM Clipper Ship model, imperfect as it is, to be extremely useful. I hope it serves you as profitably as it has others.

Uncle Eric

40

S.I.C. Codes

Dear Chris,

Know thy cones. Each area of the country has a different mix of industries and occupations. There aren't many auto parts manufacturers in Iowa, but there are plenty in Detroit. There aren't many farm equipment dealers in New York City, but there are in Nebraska. There are more fish canneries in Oregon than in Arizona, and more dude ranches in Arizona than in Baltimore.

For data processing purposes, the Federal Government classifies each industry and occupation according to **S.I.C. codes** (**Standard Industrial Classification codes**). For instance, the S.I.C. code for jewelers is 7631B; for mining engineers, 8911X; ceramics instructors, 8299D; clergy, 8665A; local government offices, 9112D; crankshaft grinders, 7538G; mailing list companies, 7331A; oil well equipment, 5082M; copper producers, 5052B; and bakery equipment manufacturers, 5081W.

Several mailing list companies specialize in printing prospect lists for any S.I.C. code in any ZIP code. If, say, you are trying to sell business equipment in Brookfield, Ohio, but you aren't having much luck, perhaps you are spending too much time trying to sell to people with empty wallets. Go to the local yellow pages and jot down a list of fifty or so of the more common types of firms in the area. The local chamber of commerce or newspaper may also have a list.

Divide the list into firms that are business cycle sensitive and insensitive, then contact a mail list company and ask for its catalog of S.I.C. lists. Go through the catalog and order the names and addresses of the S.I.C. codes with low business cycle sensitivity in your ZIP area. You can get a computer print-out, peel-and-stick mailing labels or computer disks.

If you happen to be selling something of interest to the employees rather than the firms themselves, contact the firms and ask if they have **house organ** (internal company) newsletters in which you can advertise. Do their unions have newsletters? Perhaps you can have a "special week" for the employees of these firms? Or maybe you can rent billboard space near the firms' parking lots.

Use your imagination. If DCs and ACFs exist in your area, then there is some way to contact them. Perhaps the best source of help is the Direct Marketing Association (DMA), (1120 Avenue of the Americas, New York, NY 10036-6700; phone 212-768-7277; web site: www.the-dma.org). DMA offers a small mountain of reports and how-to information to help you locate lists of the exact people you are trying to contact.

Uncle Eric

41

List Companies
and Marketing Data

Dear Chris,

If much of what we have covered so far is new to you, don't worry. You're just beginning and you have lots of time to learn. If you lend these letters to friends or relatives who are in business and they find much of this material new to them, then it's a sign they may not be familiar with the sophistication of today's computerized list companies, and they may not be tapped into the marketing data network.

Virtually all the information needed to practice BCM has already been compiled for sale, and some for free. There is a huge world-wide information industry. Contact DMA. Check the Internet.

Also ask your librarian friend to show you the DIRECT MAIL LIST CATALOG published by the Standard Rate and Data Service. This is a catalog of companies selling names and addresses of every conceivable kind of customer. They will provide you with lists custom tailored to your special needs. For instance, from one company you can get the names and addresses of:

- Individuals by sex, age and income
- Individuals by occupation
- Companies by type and size
- Customers by type of product they have purchased
- Customers by price of product they have purchased
- Customers by state, county, city, or zip code
- Stock investors
- Real estate investors
- Home owners
- And *thousands* more!

If you live in Atlanta and need to garner more DCs, the company will supply you with a list of the names and addresses of Atlanta's city clerks. If you want parks and recreation officials in Los Angeles, they can provide this, too.

If you want high income oil executives at their home addresses in Dallas, a list is available, and if you want their office addresses, this too. If you want tax shelter investors in Tampa, librarians in Los Angeles, or pawn brokers in Pittsburgh, these names and addresses are available. Anything you want, you can get.

In short, thanks to the computer, if you can find a cone, you can find and contact the people in the cone. So go to the DIRECT MAIL LIST CATALOG when you're ready to get started.

Many companies already do this on a trial and error basis. They test small samples of lists they think might work, and when a test turns out well, they rent the whole list. It's a shotgun approach. Throw lots of stuff into the marketplace in hopes that a few might hit something.

Knowing about cones and sinkholes, you can use an approach more like a rifle. You'll still need to do some experimenting, but you won't need to shoot blindly until you hit a hot spot because you know what causes hot spots and how to find them.

Uncle Eric

42

Importance of Real Estate

Dear Chris,

Real estate is the best indicator of the locations of cones and sinkholes. Where property values are skyrocketing you will find a cone, and where they are falling you will find a sinkhole.

The reason is that real estate is generally the largest purchase anyone makes. It's the largest lump of money so it brings the greatest changes.

In the early 1980s, when Detroit was in a downturn, the area's employment dropped 13% and retail sales 14%. Residential building permits dropped 76%. Dramatic. Then in the mid-1980s, Detroit began to recover. Between 1982 and 1986, building permits soared 400%.

At the same time Detroit was recovering, Houston was crashing. Houston employment dropped 5% and retail sales 13%; office construction dropped 97%.[60]

To track cones, track real estate.

---

[60] "Real Estate Advantages of Down Markets," WALL STREET JOURNAL, Oct. 16, 1989, A16.

How you do it depends on whether you are working on a national basis, state, or local. Your reference librarian should be able to point you in the direction of the best data sources.

Uncle Eric

43

Learn by Example

Dear Chris,

As the saying goes, the school of hard knocks is the best school — but the tuition is high; better to learn from the example of others.

Every business is vulnerable to downturns. After Houston's big crash in the 1980s, the city's graphic design firms were devastated. The few that survived were generally those that were lucky enough to have customers in other cities. But Creel Morell Inc. decided not to depend on luck. They developed a marketing system to protect against another downturn. Said INC. MAGAZINE:

Creel continually tracks the firm's client mix by computer, breaking down the current customer list by industry and by geographical area, and noting the percentage of the firm's overall sales represented by each large client. As cautionary measures, Creel Morrell has also raised its retainers for first-time clients (from 20% to 25% of the anticipated billing), stepped up its credit-checking procedures, and — on certain jobs — begun to demand 50% of its fee up front.

Creel not only survived, they *prospered* at a time when others in their city were going belly up; their sales *doubled* in two years.[61] A word to the wise.

Uncle Eric

---

[61] "Riding Out A Slump," INC., September 1986, p. 99.

44

Sales Side Summary

Dear Chris,

I know I'm presenting a lot of new information to you; therefore, I think a partial summary of what I've covered thus far will be helpful.

As explained in my 5th letter, the line functions of a business or home are divided into the sales functions and production functions.

Therefore, Business Cycle Management is divided into sales strategies and production strategies. We've just covered the sales side in the first 43 letters. Next, the production side.

Here is a summary for the sales side. You can apply this to your career, business, or investments.

1. Identify the sources of your income.

2. Classify these sources. Are they AC or DC? Filled or Hollow?

3. Determine how vulnerable you are. What is your mix? % of ACF, % of ACH, % of DC, % of S.

4. If you have a high concentration of ACs, try to get more DCs.

5. During economic downturns, concentrate on DCs. During booms reach out to ACs but be ready to pull back at any time. ACs are extremely vulnerable to recessions.

Chris, as I said, these strategies can apply to your investments as well as your career or business. In the mid 1990s the stock market was one of the largest ACs in history. If you had some stocks, they would have been extremely high risk, and you should have offset them by also owning a lot of DCs, meaning Treasury Bills, which are the Federal Government's IOUs backed by the printing presses.

If you are an employee instead of a business owner, it may be a good idea to ask your employers if they know about the injection effect and BCM. If they don't, pass these letters on to them, it could help make your job a lot more secure. Show them the illustrations in my previous letters. A picture is worth a thousand words.

The sooner you and everyone you depend on get in the habit of classifying people, firms and investments according to DC, ACH, ACF, and S, the sooner you will all benefit from it.

Be a clipper, follow the dancing cones.

Uncle Eric

P.S. Adopting the Super Clipper Strategy (see illustration, page 76) is not only one of the most profitable things you can do, it is one of the most noble. What the poor need most are good jobs, and good jobs come from selling products or services to people who have plenty of money to buy them.

There is simply no substitute for having the ability to stand on one's own two feet. The fastest way to raise the poor into the middle class is to link them with a cone. This is what was done for millions in the Pacific Rim countries in the 1970s, '80s and '90s. Japanese, South Koreans, Taiwanese, and many others climbed from poverty to prosperity by acquiring the ability to sell to the U.S. and other wealthy nations.

Much of this great advance was due to the invention of the container cargo ship, which greatly reduced freight rates in combination with the lowering of trade barriers. It was a repeat of the California clippers that helped ease the east coast depression by connecting the cash-hungry east coast with the goods-hungry west coast.

Chris, I know you care about people who are not as fortunate as you, and I hope that someday you will find a way to use the Super Clipper Strategy to help them.

Part 2

Production Strategy

45

Stomping the Town

Dear Chris,

Business Cycle Management is divided into sales strategies and production strategies. We're now ready to discuss production strategies.

Whenever I think about the many problems associated with production in an environment of political law, I think of the Godzilla movies. What would it be like to operate a business in Tokyo in a Godzilla movie?

Imagine the risk, the uncertainty, the stark terror. You are spending vast amounts of time and money trying to build up your firm, but you have no idea how long it will all last. You could sink millions into your factories and offices, then suddenly one day Godzilla stomps into town and smashes it all.

The last I heard, there had been some forty movies of the "Godzilla Returns" type, so the only thing a business manager in Tokyo could count on is that Godzilla would return.

That is the situation we are in today. Political law is our Godzilla, and the only thing we can count on is that Godzilla will return. He goes on unscheduled search-and-destroy missions through our cities and neighborhoods, and we have no way of knowing which ones he will smash next. How can we cope?

One way is to realize that most of mankind has lived in an environment of political law for most of history and few have ever received even the brief respite we Americans did between 1776 and the 1930s. Yet through it all, for thousands of years, some individuals have prospered. We can observe and learn their methods.

A good place to do this is in the poverty-stricken Third World countries of Latin America, Africa, and Asia. There, Godzilla sweeps through town every day, yet some entrepreneurs are still able to become wealthy. They have discovered the advantages of owning only those types of plant and equipment that can be hurriedly moved out of Godzilla's path.

Uncle Eric

46

Your Factors of Production

Dear Chris,

Earlier I pointed out that all firms are essentially production and sales, with other functions acting as support for
these two essential functions.

Economists divide the **factors of production** into four
types: **land, labor, capital,** and **entrepreneurship.** Every
asset a firm uses to produce the goods or services it sells can
be placed in one of these four categories. And every asset a
family uses to produce income can, too.

The land category can include not only terra firma, but
also the buildings, crops that might be growing on the land,
minerals in it, or the fences around it. "Land" can also
include rights to use sea lanes, or extract minerals from the
sea or from under the sea, like oil.

Labor is self explanatory.

Capital includes not only cash, but also the tools and
equipment the laborers are using. If you have a computer
you use for earning income, that's capital.

Entrepreneurship is the most important factor. The entrepreneur — and let's assume this is you — is the spark plug

that makes the machine run. You search for opportunities. You take risks. You make the important decisions and you *organize* the other three factors of production. You are the essence of the firm.

In small firms, it is usually just one or two people, the owners, who act as the entrepreneurs. In large corporations, entrepreneurship is practiced, at least in part, by all the managers and, we hope, the sales staff.

Ideally, every member of every firm would see himself as an entrepreneur working in concert with other entrepreneurs around him, but this is rarely the case. Most employees have been taught that a job is a kind of nest in which they are to be sheltered, protected, and cared for by "the company" that they see as a kind of nanny. The American heritage is indeed fading. This is no longer a nation of rugged individualists.

Chris, until my next letter, remember the four factors of production — and the need to organize them to earn income.

Uncle Eric

47

Streamlining

Dear Chris,

To minimize risks and maximize profits in an environment of political law, you must be highly adaptable, which means you must be able to move instantly and quickly whenever conditions change. This means you must be **streamlined**. You must own as little land, labor, and capital as possible. It's all excess baggage.

Ideally, in a government-controlled economy a firm should consist only of the entrepreneur and his cash, and nothing else. The entrepreneur should rent or contract for everything the firm needs or does. When Godzilla comes through town, the entrepreneur can easily fold his tent and slip away to a more promising area.

I do not know anyone who has ever managed to pare his operation down to this ideal state. Even a writer needs to own at least a few tools — paper and pencil.

But many firms in the publishing industry come close to the ideal state. People outside the publishing industry tend to envision the industry the way it was decades ago. They think of a publishing "house" where all editing, typesetting, photography, printing, binding, and sales were done under one roof.

This was my impression until a middle-sized textbook publisher asked me to write an economics text in the 1970s. The editor invited me to visit the firm, and I began looking forward to a tour of a huge building jammed with presses, typesetters, book binders, hydraulic paper cutters, and other fascinating machinery.

I found little more than a modest office building. The editor informed me that publishing "houses" are now rare, and few publishers own presses. Today, most book production tasks are purchased from outside firms specializing in these tasks. The publisher does the editing, marketing, and other "brain" work, and the outside firms handle all the physical work. In some cases the publisher even contracts for the editing, keeping only the marketing "in house."

The best streamlining example I ever saw was a publisher who ran his firm with little more than knowledge and a pile of cash. He bought a computer, but that's all. Contracting for the printing, advertising, art, editing, writing, distribution, and *everything* else, he published and sold more than 100,000 copies of a large, "slick" magazine every month, all from one room of his home. As long as his computer and phone worked, his firm worked.

In short, this entrepreneur was an *organizer and coordinator,* nothing more, and this is the ideal for which you should strive. You'll probably never reach it, but use it as your guiding star. It is safer and, in the long run, far more profitable. No sense owning a giant industrial empire when our Godzilla legal system can so easily smash it.

That's the model for a business — strive to be an organizer and coordinator, nothing more — and own nothing that will keep you from moving out of Godzilla's path. In a land of political law, the three keys to success are mobility, mobility, and mobility.

Now a few more general concepts, then we will get into specifics.

Uncle Eric

48

Cyclical Problems

Dear Chris,

Generally, it is easier to organize your factors of production if you are aware that the boom stage of the business cycle creates different types of problems than the bust stage.

When the economy is expanding, production is the major problem. You must expand fast enough to satisfy all the new demand, otherwise competitors will come in and crowd you out. This situation develops because the government can create money faster than you can create goods or services to soak up the money.

In a bust, marketing becomes the problem. Less money is being created,[62] which means less is being spent, so entrepreneurs run into problems of excess production capacity.

This is why so many firms go broke in a recession. They become ACHs (Accidental Cone Hollow). During the preceding boom they spent huge amounts of money and took on long-term commitments to produce goods or services. Then when the supply of money became restricted, they were stuck with the ability to create goods and services in

---

[62] Or demand for money has increased, which has the same effect.

quantities greater than the money flowing through their cones. Unable to cover their fixed costs, they went broke.

In other words, *bankruptcies are not made during busts, they are made during booms; they only come to light in the busts.* This means you must adopt Noah's attitude — begin building your ark while the skies are still clear and blue. Your neighbors might think you are crazy — until the rains come.

Incidentally, the government's statistics and analyses are not always accurate, which is why we can never be entirely sure whether the economy is in a boom or bust, or somewhere in between. So try talking with other business people. Are most of their problems concerned with production or with sales? If production, this indicates a boom; if sales, a bust.

Uncle Eric

49

Break-Even Analysis

Dear Chris,

In case you are not familiar with it, **break-even analysis** is one of the most tried-and-true methods for examining a firm's profitability. It divides all the firm's costs and income into three categories: **sales**, **fixed costs**, and **variable costs**. Sales needs no explanation.

Fixed costs are the costs that stay the same over a period of time. For instance, **rent**, interest payments on loans, insurance, administrative salaries, and real estate taxes are fixed costs. No matter whether the firm produces a million units or no units, these costs stay the same.

Variable costs are those that increase incrementally as units are produced. These can include raw materials, electricity, production wages, transportation, and others. These are added to the fixed costs to determine the firm's total costs. When sales reach the point where all costs (fixed and variable) are covered, this is the **break-even point**, and the firm begins earning profits with each unit sold thereafter.[63]

---

[63] Break-even analysis applies only to specific periods of time. In the long-run, all costs are variable.

Break-Even Analysis

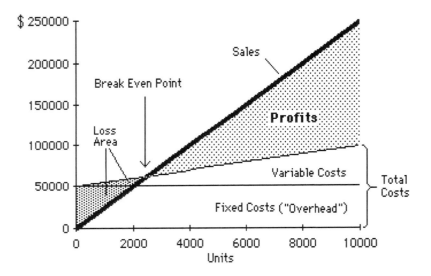

This is a typical break-even chart. When the firm's sales reach 2000 units, fixed costs are being covered. When sales reach 2250 units, all costs are covered. With the sale of the 2251st unit, the firm begins earning profits.

Yesterday's Ideal Break-Even

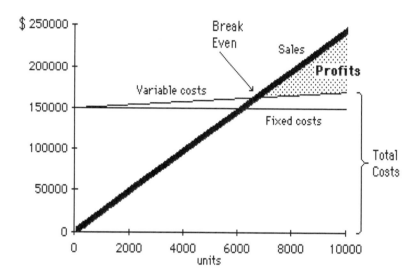

For centuries, until the 1980s, American firms would accumulate vast amounts of land, plant, and equipment for production. This is what made America an industrial giant and the land of opportunity. Break-even came late, but once a firm achieved it, profits grew rapidly. Progress was swift.

But heavy industrialization is realistic only in a country with a stable legal system. Where the law is not stable, business conditions change too rapidly for managers to plan ahead. Owning any land, plant, or equipment is a high risk.

Generally there is a trade-off between fixed costs and variable costs. In building a housing tract, the tools (capital) are part of the fixed costs. If the developer provides the workers with inexpensive hand saws and wheelbarrows, he will have low fixed costs, but more labor will be required. Wages — a variable cost — will be high.

If he provides the workers with electric saws and diesel trucks, his fixed costs will be high, but total wage expense will be lower.

If he provides enough of these kinds of sophisticated (and expensive) tools, the workers will be very efficient and their ability to produce houses will greatly increase. Production and profits might be much higher.

In America, business managers have traditionally opted for high fixed costs because sophisticated plant and equipment have long been the way to get the most production and the most profits. It is these high fixed costs that made our civilization the most advanced ever seen on earth. "High fixed costs" and "high overhead" are virtual synonyms for "industrialization."

But high fixed costs are safe only when Godzilla is not in the neighborhood. Woe unto anyone who has wealth tied up in non-portable plant and equipment when the beast is on a rampage.

This is a primary reason poverty-stricken countries are poverty-stricken. Only a high-stakes gambler owns expensive plant and equipment in a country where Godzilla roams at will. Godzilla arrived in America during the 1930s.

In a land of political law, a wise entrepreneur says to himself, "I'll let the politically naive own the plant and equipment, and I'll rent it from them when I need it. As much as possible, I will keep my fixed costs very low and sell only goods and services that can be produced with variable costs."

Chris, let me be blunt. In a land of political law, the wise entrepreneur shifts the risks of owning plant and equipment onto people who do not understand law and economics. Is this callous and cruel? Perhaps. We must face the reality that a government-controlled economy is a musical chairs economy. The factories, mines, buildings, machinery, forests, land, etc. are all necessary, but when business conditions suddenly go bad, *someone* gets caught holding the bag, *it is inescapable.* Your only choice is in deciding whether the bag holder will be you or someone else. If it's not you, then you are in a position to provide jobs, directly or indirectly, to others because of your profitability.

Most people do not have your understanding of how the world works, so you have a big advantage, your life will contain a lot less risk. When you meet someone who has been blindsided[64] by the government's economic policies, I hope you will be charitable and do your best to help them. Also, if you can see what hit them, I hope you'll explain so that they can avoid the hazard in the future.

One key to success is to acquire the attitude of the successful entrepreneurs in the Third World countries where political law is so insane they have developed cultural *traditions* against owning plant and equipment. I learned about this from Mrs. Garcia. I will tell you about her in my next letter.

Uncle Eric

---

[64] A football term meaning: to be hit on one side while looking to the other side.

50

Mrs. Garcia

Dear Chris,

In 1968, I was living in one of the few wealthy sections of Panama City, Panama, and beginning to wonder about the root cause of all the poverty I saw around me. I had traveled throughout Central America and parts of South America and had noticed there was as much poverty in the democracies as in the dictatorships.

One day I met university professor Mrs. Garcia (not her real name) and our conversation flowed to the point where I could ask her about all this. She was in a unique position to be able to answer because she was a member of one of Panama's super-wealthy ruling families.

She explained that in her country the politicians and voters believed the government should always do whatever appeared necessary to promote the common good. You might remember from our prior set of letters about political philosophies that this is **fascism.**[65] Whatever appears necessary, no exceptions, no limits.

---

[65] Uncle Eric is referring to Richard J. Maybury's book ARE YOU LIBERAL? CONSERVATIVE? OR CONFUSED? published by Bluestocking Press, web site: www.BluestockingPress.com.

Unfortunately, the politicians and voters of Panama were all human and no two ever agreed on what was good or necessary. Further, on the rare occasions when a consensus occurred, it did not last long because, being human, the politicians and voters often changed their minds.

Mrs. Garcia explained that her nation's laws changed constantly and one never knew what the government would do next. This great uncertainty created great risk for anyone investing his hard-earned money in Panama.

She said anyone intelligent enough to earn and save money was also intelligent enough to either send it out of Panama or hold it in highly portable, concealable form, such as gold, diamonds, or dollars. So, steel mills, auto plants, and other sources of jobs, production, and wealth were created in Panama only rarely, and then, in most cases, only by naive Yankees who did not understand the fickle nature of political law.

Mrs. Garcia also pointed out that the only way an owner of plant and equipment could protect his holdings from burdensome taxes, regulations, or even confiscation was by developing connections and influence in the government. Her family owned a bit of this kind of wealth because they were part of the ruling elite, but even they kept most of their wealth outside the country. She laughed, Yankees put their plant and equipment in Latin America and then are shocked to find themselves inexorably sucked into Latin American politics.

I only knew Mrs. Garcia for a few months. There was an election in 1968, and the day after the election we discovered she had vanished. I eventually learned she was not harmed, she was just facing reality. During the election, most of her relatives had been voted out of office, replaced by candidates from the other party. On the night the vote count was announced, Mrs. Garcia was seen boarding a plane.

By boarding that plane, Mrs. Garcia taught me the most important lesson in economics and business management that I have ever learned: Godzilla's behavior is not predictable, always be ready and able to get out of town fast.

That's the production side of Business Cycle Management — be ready to get out of town fast. You may never need to do it in the literal sense that Mrs. Garcia did, but your career and business operations should be structured so that Godzilla can't hurt you if he comes through your neighborhood. When the law changes and your cones dance away, you need to be able to *move* to new cones.

In my next letter we will begin getting into the practical how-to instructions.

Uncle Eric

51

A New Industry

Dear Chris,

A good rule of thumb: If it cannot be easily sold at a good price during the next recession, don't own it — rent it.

A better rule: Determine exactly what service it performs for you, then purchase this service from someone else.

Few entrepreneurs know much about political law or about cones and sinkholes, but they are learning through trial and error. More companies are beginning to realize the dangers of owning plant and equipment, and they are adopting these two rules of thumb. They are de-industrializing.

When this trend got into high gear after the 1982 recession, it generated a lot of publicity, but not much since then. Now, apparently, it is taken for granted.

A whole industry is growing up to help firms shift the risks of owning plant and equipment onto others. However, this industry is not recognized for what it is. Instead of being called the **de-industrialization** industry, it is often called restructuring, or sale-leaseback, outsourcing, vertical disaggregation, dynamic networking, or something else.

Some of the pools of naive investors buying the plant and equipment are called "vulture" funds. It is assumed that by buying and leasing back the plant and equipment to entrepreneurs, these clever investors are taking advantage of entrepreneurs. The investors believe the entrepreneurs want to retain ownership of the plant and equipment. Few of these investors realize that it may be the entrepreneurs who are the smart ones.

An offshoot of this de-industrialization industry is employee-leasing. Yes, there are now firms that hire groups of workers for other firms to rent. Decades ago there were firms that supplied temporary clerical help, and during the early 1980s this concept began spreading to the leasing of groups of unskilled laborers. Now it has progressed to the point that skilled and professional individuals — engineers, accountants, even nuclear plant designers — can be leased. Employee-leasing is one of America's fastest growing industries.

These days articles about "restructuring" and "downsizing" appear in newspapers and magazines daily, nearly every private employee lives in fear that he or she will be downsized out of a job. In a 1997 television show, Bill Cosby played a man who was downsized out of his career.

But these articles no longer talk about the causes, except to say, with a dour face, "it's good for profits."

If you want to know about the pressures that triggered the downsizing, you need to go back to when the trend was first recognized, in the mid-1980s, right after the crushing 1982 recession.

I suggest you ask a librarian for some of the articles below. As you can gather from the titles, they are revealing. And remember, most were written more than a decade ago when firms first began to realize that having permanent workers, plant, and equipment was dangerous. Godzilla is out there. The cones dance.

- "Firms Now Lease Everything But Time," U.S. NEWS & WORLD REPORT, August 14, 1989, p. 45

- "Sell the Mailroom," by Peter F. Drucker, WALL STREET JOURNAL, July 25, 1989

- "Is Your Company Too Big?" BUSINESS WEEK, March 27, 1989, p. 84

- "Utilities Learn It's Often Better To Rent," BUSINESS WEEK, February 4, 1985, p. 76

- "Surge In Restructuring Is Profoundly Altering Much Of U.S. Industry," WALL STREET JOURNAL, August 12, 1985, p. 1

- "Office Glut is Bonanza For Tenants As Landlords Cut Rents, Add Perks," WALL STREET JOURNAL, June 18, 1985, p. 33

- "Industry Cleans House," BUSINESS WEEK, November 11, 1985, p. 32

- "The Hollow Corporation," BUSINESS WEEK, March 3, 1986, p. 57-85

- "A Game For The Rich Gives Regulators The Willies," BUSINESS WEEK, August 19, 1985, p. 87

- "Facilities Design, Acquisition and Management For Privately Held Companies," INC. MAGAZINE, November 1985, p. 149

- " 'Vulture Funds' Are Forming To Snap Up Troubled Property," WALL STREET JOURNAL, November 27, 1985, p. 23

- "This Network Links Investors And Cash-Hungry Businesses," WALL STREET JOURNAL, June 3, 1985, p. 23

- "Taking Stock — Master Limited Partnerships," U.S. NEWS & WORLD REPORT, March 3, 1986, p. 60

- "Empty Industrial Plant Tests Skills Of Property Speculators," WALL STREET JOURNAL, August 21, 1985, p. 27

- "Falling Product Prices Clobber Many Firms And Force Cutbacks," WALL STREET JOURNAL, October 17, 1985, p. 1

- "Leasing People," NATION'S BUSINESS, October 1984, p. 57

- "Behind Hiring Of Temporary Employees," U.S. NEWS & WORLD REPORT, February 25, 1985, p.76

- "Professional Temps Fill Top Positions," INC. MAGAZINE, February, 1986, p. 98

- "The 'Share Economy': Can It Solve Our Economic Ills?," U.S. NEWS & WORLD REPORT, August 26, 1985, p. 65

"The Hollow Corporation" article is most revealing and contains many examples that you will understand clearly after you have finished this set of letters.

Particularly interesting in that article was the story of Galoob Toys Inc., which weathered the crushing 1982 recession without a scratch. In 1985, Galoob's sales were *ten times* those of 1981 despite the fact that, in the words of BUSINESS WEEK, "Galoob is hardly a company at all." It was mostly just a few offices full of phones and computers that were used to coordinate the activities of outside contractors.

If Galoob could do it, so can you. Their sales grew ten times those of 1981! This while the rest of the country was in the worst recession since the Great Depression.

A warning: The writers and publishers of some of those articles apparently knew little about political law. Some made impassioned pleas for a "national industrial policy" or some other kind of government "planning" to reverse the de-industrialization.

The day will certainly come when these pleas will be acted upon, so don't be led down the garden path. Remember that politicians and voters are human and they change their minds. An "industrial policy" or "plan" favorable to you this month can be suddenly transformed into one that will wipe you out next month. All we need is some kind of phony "national emergency" for all your long-term plans to become traps.

De-industrialization is caused by the *existence* of political law. We are not going to solve the problem by acquiring a greater supply of the cause.

You will not be safe making long-term investments in plant and equipment or anything else until we return to a predictable, reliable scientific legal system that does not cause the cones to dance.

Uncle Eric

The Ideal Firm
The Hollow Company

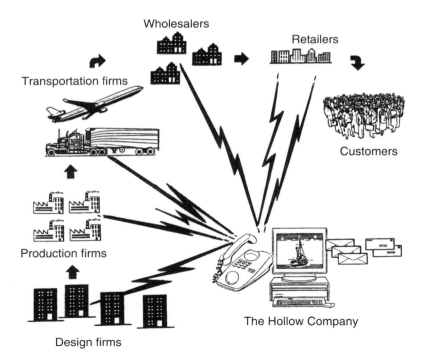

Today's Ideal Break-Even

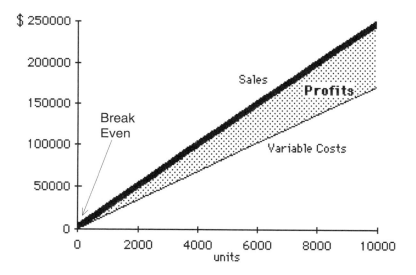

The ideal firm today is one in which all costs are variable. Without fixed costs, the firm is in a very low risk condition. When changes in law bring changes in business conditions, managers can adapt quickly, without the burden of overhead.

If you own a business or buy stock in one, this type will have less risk and probably more long-term profits than the traditional firm shown on page 197.

Note, this is an ideal. Rare is the firm that can start earning profits with its first sale. You are not likely to achieve this ideal, but it shows the direction you should be headed.

52

Break-Even Solutions

Dear Chris,

There are three ways to solve the break-even problem:

1. Use the BCM tactics I wrote about in previous letters to acquire DC sources of income. If you have enough DCs, they will hold your income above your break-even point even during a severe recession. This is a good tactic, but for many firms and individuals it is difficult to do, DCs might be scarce.

2. Make your break-even point flexible so that if income slides downward you can slide your break-even point downward, too. This is the ideal tactic but few of us can slide our break-even points down to zero, renting absolutely everything we need. (See the illustrations for the ideal company on pages 208 and 209). We cannot convert *all* fixed costs to variable costs, so...

3. Use a combination of #1 and #2. Make your break-even point as flexible as possible and use #1 to cover whatever is inflexible.

Business Cycle Management
Break-Even Analysis

Compromise Solution

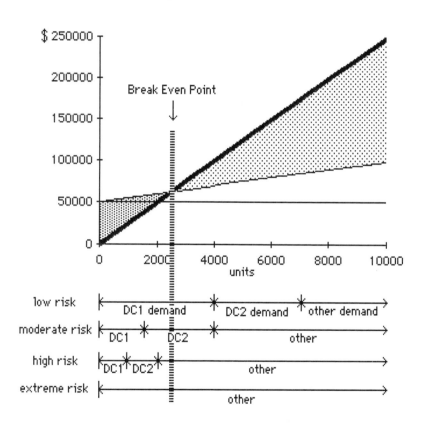

If the firm can acquire enough DC1 customers for DC1 demand alone to hold sales above break-even, the firm will be in a low-risk condition.

The remainder of these letters will suggest various ways to get rid of plant and equipment, and convert fixed costs to variable costs.

But before we get into **break-even flexibility**, let's make sure you really need it. Who are your sources of income? How many of them are DCs? If, for instance, you own a store in a retirement community (lots of Social Security income), you may have so many DCs that you are solidly above your break-even point and in a very low-risk condition. You may be virtually Godzilla-proof.

Similarly, if you are located near the large Neiman Marcus store at the point where Washington, D.C. meets Bethesda, MD, you may have plenty of DCs. Thanks to the nearby federal bureaucracy, this geographic spot is one of the most affluent in the nation. Even in the depths of the 1982 recession, 18.3% of the families in the Washington-Bethesda area were earning more than $50,000 per year. This while families in metropolitan areas nationwide who earned more than $50,000 averaged only 6.7%.

Said U.S. NEWS & WORLD REPORT at that time,[66] "The government spread $603.6 billion across the U.S. last year — an average of $2,591 for each man, woman, and child. The census bureau reported that Washington, D.C. received more per capita than any state, $17,127." The closest runner-up was Alaska at $4,533.

Washington, D.C. has long been the healthiest Deliberate Cone in the world.

But if your customer base is not in these types of favored locations, you will need to restructure your factors of production. More rules of thumb:

---

[66] February 14, 1983.

1. Don't buy a business building or home, rent it. This way, if a recession or some other political catastrophe cuts your income, you can move to a smaller, less expensive structure.

2. In your business, use equity financing rather than debt financing. Sell stock or take on limited partners. If you must use debt financing, use it only for variable costs — inventory, for instance. When a recession hits and sales drop off, you can reduce your debt burden along with sales.

3. Do not get involved in any project that will take more than a year to go all the way to completion. Many firms get into trouble by launching long-term projects that make sense when monetary policy is loose but turn catastrophic when it becomes tight. (Remember, *bankruptcies are made during booms, they only come to light in busts.* It is during the booms that the Accidental Cones grow huge and lure in businesses.)

4. Make a conscious effort to be on the other side of this long-term risk situation. During periods of prosperity, build a reserve of liquid capital — cash, Treasury Bills, etc. Then when the next recession hits and your more aggressive competitors start going belly up because their overhead is too high, you can buy their fixed assets at greatly reduced prices. You will grow your business and they will be grateful for the sale. Use their assets for your own operation until the next boom develops, then sell out during the boom when prices are high.

Unless your income is solidly DC, own nothing that ties you down. In a government-controlled economy, anything that requires a concrete foundation is a trap.

The exception to this rule has to do with something called **payback analysis**, which I'll discuss in detail in a future letter.

Without DCs, every part of your business, career, and home should be something that can be put on wheels or quickly and easily sold within days. If you absolutely cannot get along without something that is fixed and highly illiquid[67], sell it and lease it back from the buyer.

Suppose you own a lumber mill and forest. Sell both the mill and forest to an investor who does not agree with your view of the future. In the deal, include an agreement allowing you to rent the use of the mill and forest. The investor will feel he is getting a valuable property with an automatic income, but you know that as soon as monetary policy tightens, you can walk away from the whole thing if necessary. In short, if he wants to take the risk of being caught holding the bag, that's up to him.

Again, political law exists, and it changes the locations of the cones. We cannot do anything about that. *Someone* will get caught holding the bag. Make sure it's not you.

And warn everyone you care about.

Uncle Eric

---

[67] Difficult to sell.

53

The Most Risky Investment

Dear Chris,

Many Americans have a fixation about real estate, they think it's a magic investment that can't lose. In a country where the law is reasonably stable this attitude may be fine, but not in America today. Business conditions change too fast — you may not be able to sell out in time.

If you own real estate, it might make you rich, but it also might make you broke. Remember Houston and Denver. There is little to keep it from happening anywhere in the U.S. at any time.

Being the most illiquid investment, real estate is also the most risky.

If your real estate is in a very stable Deliberate Cone — a high income retirement community for instance — it might be profitable and low risk, but do your homework. Be very certain your cone will not dance away.

Uncle Eric

54

Specialization

Dear Chris,

The principle that economists call **specialization of labor** is one of the primary keys to individual success and to a nation's advancement in an environment of **scientific law.** But in an environment of political law it is dangerous.

Rather than view yourself as a butcher, baker, or candlestick maker, view yourself as a professional *entrepreneur* who sometimes sells meat, other times bread, and other times candles, depending on what Godzilla has been up to lately. Whatever the cones want to buy, you sell.

If you want a profession that is necessarily highly specialized — say dentistry — then be a part-time entrepreneur who takes advantage of whatever opportunities happen to be promising at the moment.

In an environment of political law, *the big dollars are earned by the traders, not the producers.* The producers are Godzilla-fodder.

Uncle Eric

55

Payback Analysis

Dear Chris,

One of the most helpful concepts to understand is payback analysis. Payback is the time required to recover the cost of a specific investment.

Let's say you buy a machine you believe will be productive enough to pay for itself in three years. This means its expected payback is 33% (1÷3 years = 33%). That's like investing $1,000, and each year for three years, getting back $333.33.

If it will pay for itself in two years, its payback will be 50%. (1 ÷ 2 = 50%). That's like investing $1,000, and each year for two years, getting back $500.

The higher the payback percentage, the less risk because you get your money back faster. A 100% payback means you get all your money back in one year; 200% means six months.

Generally, in a business, earlier investments have better paybacks than later investments. For instance, when you first buy your computer, the efficiency it adds to your organization may cause its payback to be very short. My first computer boosted my productivity so much it paid for itself in three months — a payback of 400% (1÷0.25 years = 400%).

At a time when Treasury Bills were paying 10%, this was a most attractive investment.

But each upgrade to increase the capacity of the computer has a smaller payback and is harder to justify. In my business, when payback drops to 50% (two years), I say no. Business conditions can change so much in two years that the risk of a 50% payback is too high for the equipment to be attractive to me.

I expect that eventually government officials will be desperately changing their laws and policies — and the locations of the cones — often enough for a 200% payback to be unattractive. We will be in a condition of runaway de-industrialization.

Chris, in general, the less DC income you have, the more you will need higher paybacks in order to keep your risks down. If, say, you are dependent entirely on ACs, and you are buying business equipment or making other investments that have only 10% paybacks, the next recession could reduce your income long before you've gotten your money back from your investments. You could run entirely out of money. Not good. Look for high paybacks.

Uncle Eric

56

Start-Up Firms: An Example

Dear Chris,

When you are ready to launch your business, here is an example of how to use BCM to get off on the right foot.

Let's say you were the manager of a copper mine in Colorado, but the 1980 and '82 recessions were so hard on the copper industry that your mine was closed in 1983.

It is now December 1985 and you have been out of work for two years. The entire region around your home is severely depressed, it is a sinkhole.

Waiting for the recovery to arrive, you have been tinkering in your kitchen and invented a new kind of breakfast cereal, which you call Yummy Gobblies. The cereal is great and you believe it can make you a fortune, but how do you produce and sell it?

According to America's Horatio Alger tradition, you would pool all your money along with that of friends, and perhaps some you've borrowed from a bank, and set up the Yummy Gobblies Company. You'd rent an office, hire a secretary, and buy a factory building and the necessary equipment. (You can get these cheap because your entire region is depressed and the present owners are in need of cash and anxious to sell.)

Then, according to tradition, you'd hire a dozen or so employees. As they are producing the first batch of cereal, you'd market to surrounding counties to get orders from grocery store buyers. Your hope would be that Yummy Gobblies will become so popular you can eventually spread into surrounding states, and someday the entire country.

Forget it. If the Fed tightens its monetary policy, the price of copper will fall further, more people in your region will become unemployed, and more food stores will go out of business. The fledgling demand for your cereal will go into a tailspin and you will be in hock for the rest of your life.

Use BCM instead. *Do not begin with production, begin with sales.* Put your new cereal formula on a back shelf for a while and start doing research. Find a solid, healthy cone. In 1985, Sacramento would have been a good one.

Then research this cone until you know everything there is to know about it. Find the hot spots — the neighborhoods where per capita income is high, unemployment is low and, where possible, a large percentage of the people are DCs. Then write the Sacramento phone company and get a Sacramento phone book. Phone all the food stores in the hot spots and make appointments to meet with the buyers.

Make up some product samples, then drive to Sacramento and meet with the buyers to get orders. Do all this before you've produced even one case of Yummy Gobblies.

Return home and meet with the owners of the factory and production equipment. Don't buy the factory and equipment, just show the owners your orders and tell them you'd like them to produce the cereal according to specifications you will provide.

Don't buy trucks. Arrange for a trucking company to deliver the raw materials to the factory and to pick up the finished product and haul it to Sacramento.

To develop a strong and reliable demand in Sacramento, send coupons to households in the hot spots. To do this, contact list brokers and give them the target zip codes. Ask for lists of government employees living in these areas. Time your mailing so that the coupons arrive in the Sacramento mailboxes a few days after the product arrives in the stores.

To boost demand, you might also ask for lists of pregnant mothers in hot spot neighborhoods. You will not only bring in the mothers, but when the children grow old enough to eat Yummy Gobblies, you will automatically get an increased demand from them.

The names and addresses of the pregnant mothers will cost about $100 per 1000. The way the list companies compile them is by following the paper trail of the pregnant mothers. When a woman buys a dress at a maternity shop, enrolls in a childbirth training class, sees her obstetrician or gynecologist, or signs up for a diaper service, her name and address may be sold to a list company. There are even companies that specialize in mailing large packages of coupons to pregnant mothers. For a comparatively small fee you can have your coupons included in these packages.

In short, don't spend your limited capital on production, spend it on sales. Don't buy plant, equipment, and labor — rent it; use the money you save to *sell* the product to cones. That's how you avoid becoming an ACH.

Uncle Eric

57

Careers in BCM

Dear Chris,

Now that you understand BCM, consider setting up your own BCM consulting firm.

Difficult as it may be to believe, most American business people still do not know about Godzilla. They know about the creature's work — they see recessions, bankruptcies, unemployment, and poverty springing up all around them — but they do not know about the creature itself. Not knowing about political law, they do not know how to adapt to its presence. They just establish their careers, investments, and businesses on the assumption that if they are honest and hard working the turmoil will not strike them. They do not appreciate the fact that Godzilla doesn't care how honest and hard working they are, he's *hungry!*

Since the only thing we can be sure of is that Godzilla will return, I can think of no type of firm likely to be as profitable as a Godzilla-protection agency — a firm that performs BCM for other firms.

There is no need to do everything described in my letters. Just start by doing one or two, then branch out as you become more experienced.

For instance, you might start by offering the service of customer classification. Point out to your clients that some of their customers have more stable, reliable incomes than others. County employees, for example, have more stable, reliable incomes than auto workers or farmers. Your clients already know this, so you only need to draw it to their attention, then ask if they would like for you to classify their customers so they will know how stable and reliable their firm's sales are, and what type of customers they should be gathering. Do they have enough Deliberate Cones to safely reach out for Accidental Cones, or should they garner more Deliberates? Your classification service will help them decide.

Unless you have a $15 million Cray supercomputer, you won't be able to fully classify and describe every market in the country, but you don't need to. Start locally, then spread out to larger and larger surrounding areas.

Here is a telling remark printed in the catalog of one of the nation's largest mail list companies: "Don't buy our lists for an area you already know well. We can't possibly keep track of business changes in your local area as well as you can. You'll hear about start-ups and failures long before we will." Start local.

You might want to start a local area BCM newsletter. Or you might want to become a list manager for lists of DCs and ACs, or even a broker or clearinghouse for lists of DCs and ACs.

To begin your own list of local area firms and individuals classified by cone and business cycle sensitivity, check STANDARD AND POOR'S REGISTER OF CORPORATIONS, DIRECTORS AND EXECUTIVES. This register provides more than 45,000 company profiles and 400,000 names and addresses of executives. It gives you sales volume, S.I.C. codes, ZIP codes, and much more. Look it over at your local library. You can also get this same kind of information from Dun & Bradstreet.

On your computer create street maps of the local area. On the street maps you can put symbols designating the types of cones, business cycle sensitivity, and exact locations of a firm's customers. Retailers could use the maps to see which geographic areas their marketing has or has not penetrated.

Finding clients who need your help should be quite simple. Just drive around your local area looking for office buildings, factories, stores, and other types of plant and equipment. Wherever you find this expensive, non-portable wealth you have found someone who does not know about Godzilla, or about cones and sinkholes.

Chris, the cost of computers has fallen so much that you may be able to develop an extremely sophisticated application of BCM. I once saw a meteorology program adapted for use in oceanography. This program was originally intended to show a three-dimensional moving color picture of a weather system in action — jet streams, thunderstorms, updrafts, clouds, rain, etc. The oceanographer had adapted it to show the ocean bottom and the currents, eddies and whirlpools flowing along the East Coast.

If such programs can be adapted for use in oceanography, I do not see why they could not also be used for marketing. A BCM firm could maintain a data base on a given geographic or demographic part of the country, then enter data relating to a specific firm. The picture would show the firm's location in the cone/sinkhole landscape.

By entering data from several previous years, a moving picture could show the area's history, and the firm's history — how it got to where it is.

Then the picture could switch to showing a recommended location for the firm, and the "tubing" (transportation and communication avenues) the firm could use to connect recommended cones to recommended sinkholes. It would not work for firms that have customers that cannot be identified, but I'm sure it would work for many firms.

The possibilities are exciting, and I suspect a teenager could do a basic version on his home computer.

I'd start with Matthew Lesko's LESKO'S INFO-POWER (web site: www.Matthew-Lesko.com)

As I said in an earlier letter, the U.S. Department of Labor keeps track of the amount of jobs in various industrial sectors — banking, county government, food stores, mining, manufacturing, you name it — on a local and state basis.

The data I acquired from the Labor Department gave a very clear picture of the demographic cones and sinkholes. Census data would give you a picture of the geographic ones.

I was amazed at how well it worked, and I cannot see why you couldn't do it, too. It's not hard for someone who is an experienced computer user — just time consuming, and I believe there is a fortune in it.

Chris, a recent study of America's millionaires shows that 80% of them earned their money themselves, they did not inherit it, and most did it not by investing, but by owning a business.[68]

You can start a business at any time in your life, Chris. Get a BCM service up and running and advertise it on the Internet. Good luck!

Uncle Eric

---

[68] "The Rich Aren't So Different After All," by Anita Sharpe, WALL STREET JOURNAL, November 12, 1996, p. B1.

58

Investment Strategy

Dear Chris,

At some point you will have enough money — after your BCM firm is going great guns — that you will need to devote significant time and energy to managing the money. You might be told that you should have a long-term plan.

Your long-term investment plan should be to have no long-term plan. The flows of money are no longer predictable enough. We now live in a world where we must continually pursue new cones while swerving to avoid sinkholes.

Even some of the long-stable federal cones are becoming unstable. Officials are closing hospitals, military bases, and regulatory agencies. Federal cones remain more stable than most others, but not as stable as in the past.

A good general rule is, don't get into anything you can't get out of fast. You will need to occasionally make exceptions, but the more closely you can follow this rule, the less often you will be mired in a sinkhole. Look out for those ACs, especially ACFs.

Here is a six-step plan.

1. Segregate your assets into savings and speculation. The purpose of savings is capital preserva-
   tion to keep what you have. In the savings category, safety is paramount, income secondary. I
   like Treasury Bills (T-Bills).

2. Split the money you've allocated for speculation
   into "hold" and "committed." "Hold" is money
   you aren't using yet. It should be parked in highly
   liquid, highly safe media. Again, I like T-Bills or
   money market funds that invest solely in T-Bills
   and other short-term federal instruments.

3. Commit funds for speculation only when you are
   sure you have located a cone. This is very important. *No longer see yourself as investing in stocks,
   bonds, real estate, or whatever. See yourself as
   investing in cones.*

   In other words, you might locate one cone that's a
   stock, another that's a bond and another that's a
   precious metal. What it is on the surface isn't very
   important, just do your best to make certain it's a
   growing cone.

4. Determine the cone's characteristics. Is it Deliberate or Accidental? Hollow or Filled? What is
   it's probable longevity?

5. Always be diversified, never put all your eggs in
   one basket. This means also never commit all
   your funds to one nation. Diversification across

borders is as important as diversification across investments. Switzerland is the safest place on earth. Consider New Zealand, too.

6. Establish a regular routine for tracking the health of your cones. You might want to create a weekly or monthly checklist of indicators for tracking the flow of money. Whatever data you used to determine the cone's characteristics (see #4) should be on this checklist.

By the way, Chris, diversification applies to your own talents and skills as well. Have a multitude of skills you can rely on should the economy suddenly change, so your work or career can change with it. I once knew an individual who earned his living as a presidential speech writer. Unfortunately, the candidate for whom he worked lost the election and my friend was out of work — as a presidential speech writer. Being a man of diversified talents, however, he worked for some time as a welder.

Uncle Eric

59

Two Types of Investment Cones

Dear Chris,

Investments come in two types, Double Cone and Single Cone. A **Double Cone Investment** is one that earns profits through two flows of money — **capital gains** and earnings. Examples of doubles are stocks, bonds, and commercial real estate. All earn money through their daily operations, and we also hope they rise in value, earning more money through capital gains. A capital gain is an increase in the value of the investment, as when a stock rises.

Single Cone Investments are those that earn profits only through capital gains. Examples are commodities, undeveloped land, currencies, art, and antiques.

In most cases, the profit-potential of earnings is smaller than that of capital gains, but it can also be more stable and less risky. When you hear of someone who made a killing in an investment, it's almost always through a capital gain, not earnings. And when you've heard of someone who took a bath, it's almost always from a capital loss, not an earnings loss.

Earnings can be either Deliberate or Accidental Cones. A capital gain is an Accidental Cone, and I cannot think of any exceptions to that.

When you are pursuing a capital gain, you are betting you have spotted a growing Accidental Cone.

Very important: A capital gain Accidental Cone is likely to be emotion-laden, caused by the herd mentality, the band wagon effect. In its early stages an Accidental Cone may be growing for realistic reasons, but when the herd spots it and climbs on, reason goes out the door. You can make enormous profits in one of these emotional Accidental Cones, but get out before the herd does.

How do you know when the herd will get out? You don't. There is an old story: Someone once asked the wealthy financier Baron Rothschild how he got rich and he said, "I always bought too late and sold too early." In other words, he *avoided losses* by being cautious. He knew that getting out a year too early is better than getting out a day too late.

My experience has been that these hyper-inflated emotional Accidental Cones are glamour-driven. The stock market of the 1920s and 1990s, and California ("Golden State") real estate in the 1970s and 1980s, are two examples. Where you see a large cone surrounded by flash and pizzazz, you will also find large profits — as long as you bail out before everyone else does.

The heavier the Fed's expansion of the money supply, the more bloated the Accidental Cones. And the more fragile.

Uncle Eric

60

Summary

Dear Chris,

Economics is often thought to be highly mathematical, a mass of boring charts, graphs, and statistics. Most people study economics for the first time in high school, and being completely baffled by it, avoid any further contact with it for the rest of their lives. Consequently, they become victims of the economic chaos that results from a government-controlled economy. They wander through their career and financial lives totally at the mercy of the business cycle. Because I don't want this to happen to you, I wrote this set of letters to explain the strategy you need to cope with, and prosper from, the government's injection of new money into the economy — a strategy I call Business Cycle Management.

Chris, in my first letter I mentioned that in explaining the injection effect and Business Cycle Management, I was trying to do what some would say cannot be done without using a lot of calculus. But, as you know, I firmly believe any subject can be understood if it is explained well. I chose to use historical examples and illustrations. I hope it worked. If anything remains unclear, please let me know.

Let these letters sit for a couple of weeks so the ideas can simmer, then reread them. Now that you have the whole model in your head, you will find more useful ideas because you will be able to see many interrelationships that were not apparent on the first reading. The economy is an organic system where all parts are connected to all other parts, the opportunities to profit from these connections are limitless.

Chris, this set of letters about cones is an example of the importance of insisting on clear, accurate definitions of words.

The common definition of inflation is "rising prices."

The real definition is *"an increase in the money supply that causes* rising prices."

A person who accepts the common definition will have little chance of understanding the cones or their effect on his career, business, and investments, for he will not know the importance of money supply.

In other words, this is a case where a poor definition of a single word can leave a person confused and defenseless for his entire life. But a clear, accurate definition can open up a world of opportunities.

Most government schools teach Keynesian economics, which promotes the common definition. Rising prices puts the blame for inflation on the business community for increasing the price of goods and services.

Where does the responsibility for inflation lie, given the real definition?

According to the Constitution, who has the legal right to print money?

Why would government schools promote the common definition? Think about it.

Before I finish this final letter, here are eight points summarizing all these letters:

1. When the government injects money into the economy, the money goes somewhere and causes changes. Economists call this the injection effect.

2. One kind of change is a *Deliberate* Cone or hot spot. This is a geographic area or demographic group receiving money according to a specific government plan.

3. Another is an *Accidental* Cone or hot spot. This is a geographic area or demographic group receiving a flow of money guided by unpredictable forces. Often money flows into an Accidental Cone simply because whatever is in the cone has become fashionable.

4. Fashion changes, usually unpredictably.

5. So Deliberates are more stable than Accidentals. But Accidentals tend to be more bloated and profitable.

6. Entrepreneurs know hot spots develop, but few understand why. They try to predict the locations of new hot spots. In these locations they place new plant and equipment expecting they'll be able to sell the products once the demand develops.

7. If they are right, they have created a *Filled* Cone — a structure of plant and equipment with money flowing through it — and they earn income from

this Filled Cone for as long as the flow of money lasts. If they are wrong, their cone remains *Hollow* and they go broke.

8. Never *assume* any hot spot will be long-lived. Research it. To be prosperous and *stay* that way, always be ready to follow the dancing cones.

Chris, I suggest that you dog-ear this page and all the illustration pages, then establish a life-long practice for yourself. Each year on your birthday, as a way to judge the stability of your situation at that time, review these eight points and the illustrations. I believe they will remain relevant for the rest of your life. An annual reminder will save you a lot of grief, and hopefully, open your eyes to a lot of opportunities.

Remember, Chris, the economy is not a machine. It is an ecology made of biological organisms — humans. It is far too complex for any government to fully understand or improve, but governments try to do this. They play God. The result is bankruptcies, unemployment and poverty for millions of good people who have never harmed anyone. An ACH (Accidental Cone Hollow) is a terrible disaster.

However, in good times and bad, someone is always earning money. As I said in my first letter, even in the Great Depression, some people not only got by, they got rich.

And the reason? They followed the dancing cones produced by the injection effect. Always be ready to switch to a new cone.

I cannot exaggerate the dangers of assuming your cones will remain stable. *Every expansion of the money supply causes malinvestment.* Each injection creates *traps* that ruin

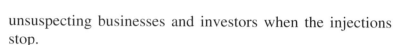

unsuspecting businesses and investors when the injections stop.

The speed and severity of a collapse can be awesome. In 1929 and 1987, the stock market cone collapsed in just hours.

Agricultural markets were major Accidental Cones in the 1970s. As money flowed to farmers, Iowa's average net farm income in 1981 was $17,700. Then federal officials tightened their monetary policy and in *one year* Iowa's farm income plunged to only $7,400. A year after that, it had become a *negative* $1,900. In just 24 months, these innocent people went from a raging boom to crushing disaster.

Nine years later they had not recovered. When the Fed began its new injections in 1983, the new money went into stocks, California real estate, and many other cones, but not to farmers. Their cone had been flattened. Thousands of fine people who had never harmed anyone were ruined.

Chris, returning to the question of ethics discussed in my second letter, once you are using BCM you will earn wealth from the injection effect, and you may be tempted to see the injection effect as a good thing. You might even want it to continue and grow.

Do all you can to avoid this temptation. Continually remind yourself that the injection effect is evil, and help others understand how it affects them. Never do anything that would preserve or increase the injection effect.

Bear in mind that when a new cone develops, there may be more money in this location, but this does not increase the total amount of *real* wealth in the society — the food, cars, homes, clothing, etc. It just attracts wealth from other areas, and some of these areas become sinkholes. The money cone is a wealth *magnet* not a wealth creator. *The people, buildings, machines, and other productive things in a cone would be in other places producing other things if they had not been lured into the cone by the money. They are not invest-ment, they are malinvestment.*

If you do something to create a Deliberate Cone, you are hurting people somewhere, by attracting wealth away from them; good intentions do not prevent the damage. Remember our hamburger stand example and the principle of marginal-ity.

Do have a career or business that taps into existing cones. I cannot see that you have much choice in the matter, the cone/sinkhole landscape is the economic environment in which you must live. Also, you have a responsibility to support yourself and eventually, perhaps, a family. Through your own success you may even provide employment for others, directly or indirectly. Perhaps the most ethical ap-proach is to try to tap into existing ACs and avoid DCs, I don't know. But I do know you should not do anything to make the cone/sinkhole landscape worse. And I hope you will warn others about it.

Chris, you might consider lending this set of letters (as well as my previous sets of letters on economics and law) to people you care about. Even though these people may appear to be wildly successful, and I hope they are, they need to know how to stay that way by learning everything they can about Business Cycle Management — the Clipper Ship Strat-egy.

Remember, Chris: Be a Clipper.

Uncle Eric

Spread the Word!

Be a Clipper!

If all prices and incomes rose equally, no harm would be done to any one. But the rise is not equal. Many lose and some gain.

—Irving Fisher
writing about inflation in
STABILIZING THE DOLLAR, 1920

Government is the great fiction, through which everybody endeavours to live at the expense of everybody else.

— Frederic Bastiat (1801-1850)
ESSAYS ON POLITICAL ECONOMY, 1872

Appendix

Bibliography

- A TIME FOR TRUTH by William E. Simon, published by Berkley Publishing. Out of Print.

- ALL SAIL SET: THE GRIPPING AND AUTHENTIC YARN OF A RACE 'ROUND THE HORN ON BOARD THE GREATEST CLIPPER EVER BUILT—THE FLYING CLOUD by Armstrong Sperry, published by David R. Godine, MA. For ages 10 and up. Historical fiction.

- ARE YOU LIBERAL? CONSERVATIVE? OR CONFUSED? by Richard J. Maybury, published by Bluestocking Press (web site: www.BluestockingPress.com).

- BETTER THAN A LEMONADE STAND by Daryl Bernstein, published by Beyond Words Publishing, Inc., Hillsboro, OR.

- BY THE GREAT HORNSPOON by Sid Fleischman (for ages 9 and up), published by Little Brown, NY. Historical fiction.

- CAPITALISM FOR KIDS by Karl Hess, published by Bluestocking Press (web site: www.BluestockingPress.com).

- CLIPPER SHIP an I Can Read® book by Thomas P. Lewis, (for ages 7-9), published by HarperTrophy, NY. Historical fiction.

- DIRECT MAIL LIST CATALOG, published by Standard Rate and Data Service.

- ECONOMIC TRENDS, Federal Reserve Bank of Cleveland, Box 6387, Cleveland, OH 44101.

• FEDERAL BUSINESS OPPORTUNITIES (www.fedbizopps.gov).

• FEDERAL STATISTICAL DATA BASES by William R. Evinger, published by Oryx Press, 2214 North Central At Encanto, Phoenix, AZ 85004.

• FREE MARKET ECONOMICS: SELECTED ARTICLES FROM A BASIC READER, by Bettina B. Greaves, published by Bluestocking Press (web site: www.BluestockingPress.com).

• FREE TO CHOOSE by Milton Friedman, published by Harcourt, Brace & Co., CA.

• THE GREAT SHIPS: THE CLIPPERS. A video about clipper ships that has excellent economic history. Available from The History Channel, 1-800-708-1776.

• INVESTMENT BANKING by Rachel S. Epstein, published by Chelsea House Publishers, NY.

• LESKO'S INFO-POWER III by Matthew Lesko,published by Invisible Ink Press (see www.Matthew-Lesko.com).

• THE MYTH OF THE ROBBER BARRONS by Burton W. Folsom, Jr., published by Young America's Foundation, Herndon, VA.

• STANDARD AND POOR'S REGISTER OF CORPORATIONS, DIRECTORS AND EXECUTIVES, published by Standard and Poor's.

• STATISTICAL ABSTRACT OF THE UNITED STATES, Superintendent of Documents, Mail Stop: SSOP, Washington, D.C. 20402.

- STORY OF AMERICAN RAILROADS, THE by Stewart H. Holbrook, published by Crown, a division of Random House, NY.

- UNCLE ERIC TALKS ABOUT PERSONAL, CAREER, AND FINANCIAL SECURITY, revised edition (2004), by Richard J. Maybury, published by Bluestocking Press (web site: www.BluestockingPress.com).

- U.S. FINANCIAL DATA, published by the Federal Reserve Bank of St. Louis, Box 442, St. Louis, MO 63166.

- WALL STREET: HOW IT WORKS and WHAT IS A SHARE OF STOCK? by Jeffrey B. Little, published by Chelsea House Publishers, NY.

- WHATEVER HAPPENED TO JUSTICE? by Richard J. Maybury, published by Bluestocking Press (web site: www.BluestockingPress.com).

- WHATEVER HAPPENED TO PENNY CANDY? by Richard J. Maybury, published by Bluestocking Press (web site: www.BluestockingPress.com).

- YOUNG ENTREPRENEUR'S GUIDE TO STARTING AND RUNNING A BUSINESS by Steve Mariotti, published by Times Business, NY.

- YOUNG INVESTOR, THE, by Katherine R. Bateman, published by Chicago Review Press Chicago, IL.

Contact your librarian or a used bookstore for locating out-of-print books.

Book Suppliers

Bluestocking Press: web site: www.bluestockingPress.com (For additional contact information, see the last page of this book.)

Foundation for Economic Education, 30 South Broadway, Irvington-on-Hudson, NY 10533. Phone: 800-452-3518 or 914-591-7230. web site: www.fee.org

Laissez Faire Books, 7123 Interstate 30, Suite 42, Little Rock, AR, 72209. Phone: 800-326-0996 or 501-975-3650. web site: www.lfb.com

The Liberator Catalog, Advocates for Self-Government, Inc., 5 South Public Square, Suite 304, Cartersville, GA 30120. Phone: 800-932-1776 or 770-386-8372. web site: www.self-gov.org

Liberty Tree Network. 100 Swan Way, Oakland, CA, 94621-1428. Phone: 800-927-8733 or 510-632-1366. web site: www.liberty-tree.org

Glossary

AC. Abbreviation for Accidental Cone.

ACCIDENTAL CONE. A cone produced accidentally by the government's fiscal, monetary or regulatory policies.

ACCIDENTAL CONE EXPORTER. A cone produced accidentally by the government's fiscal, monetary, or regulatory policies, which derives its income from sales abroad.

ACCIDENTAL CONE FILLED. A cone that has lots of money running through it.

ACCIDENTAL CONE HOLLOW. A cone with plant, equipment, and workers but little money.

ACCIDENTAL CONE IMPORTER. A cone produced accidentally by the government's fiscal, monetary, or regulatory policies, which derives its income from sales of goods purchased abroad.

ACE. Abbreviation for Accidental Cone Exporter.

ACF. Abbreviation for an Accidental Cone Filled.

ACH. Abbreviation for an Accidental Cone Hollow.

ACI. Abbreviation for Accidental Cone Importer.

ANOMALY. A strange exception to what would be expected.

APPLICATION. Practice in the real world.

AUSTRIAN ECONOMICS. The most free-market of all the economic viewpoints today. The origin was in Vienna, Austria, but the country where it is most popular today is probably the U.S. Austrian economists have won Nobel Prizes, and the most widely known Austrian economist, F.H. Hayek, was highly influential in the economic policies of British Prime Minister Margaret Thatcher. Austrian economics sees the economy not as a machine, but as an almost infinitely complex ecology made of biological organisms — humans.

BCM. See Business Cycle Management.

BEAR MARKET. A falling market. Opposite of a bull market.

BLOATED CONES. A cone so packed with money that it contains a huge amount of malinvestment.

BOOM-AND-BUST BUSINESS CYCLE. The so-called business cycle. The pattern of inflationary economic expansions alternating with deflationary contractions (recessions and depressions).

BREAK-EVEN ANALYSIS. Mathematical calculation showing the point at which a company's costs and income are exactly equal, the break-even point.

BREAK-EVEN FLEXIBILITY. Making one's break-even point flexible so that if income slides downward, the break-even point can be slid downward, too.

BREAK-EVEN POINT. When sales reach the point where all costs are covered and the firm begins earning profits with each unit sold thereafter.

BULL MARKET. A strongly rising market. Opposite of a bear market.

BUSINESS CYCLE. The "boom-and-bust" cycle of inflationary expansions and deflationary contractions or recessions.

BUSINESS CYCLE INSENSITIVE. Income only slightly affected by the boom-and-bust cycle.

BUSINESS CYCLE MANAGEMENT. An investment strategy that shows business managers and sales people how to take advantage of the fact that pockets of prosperity can be discovered and tapped into, no matter how good or bad business conditions may be.

CAPITAL. Capital is the buildings, office equipment, and other tools workers need to produce what we want to buy. Or, the money saved to buy these things.

CAPITAL GAIN. A capital gain is an increase in the value of the investment, as when a stock rises.

CAPITALISM. A term coined by Socialist Karl Marx, who meant the stage of economic development in which large amounts of capital (tools) are accumulated by private firms. Today capitalism is generally taken to mean free markets, free trade, and free enterprise. The economic philosophy of the right.

CAPITALIST. One who believes in capitalism.

CARTEL. Independent commercial enterprises that combine for the purpose of limiting competition.

CLIPPER SHIP STRATEGY. Find out where there is a pile of money, tap into that pile, and don't expect the pile to last forever. Always be searching for new piles.

COLD SPOT. An area where sales are slack and incomes low. An area of depressed economic activity.

COMMODITIES. Raw materials. Natural resources. Basic materials traded on commodity markets. Examples: copper, lumber, soybeans, oil, gold, silver, aluminum, wheat, corn.

COMMODITY MARKETS. Where raw materials are bought and sold.

CONE. An area where money is flowing in large quantities and firms are placing plant and equipment to tap into these flows.

DANCING CONE. A cone that moves to another location.

DC. Abbreviation for a deliberate cone.

DCF1. A Deliberate Cone, Federally created and *first (1st) in line* at the federal spigot (which is backed by the federal printing press.) These are people who have extremely steady, reliable incomes. Examples are retirees receiving Social Security, military pensioners, and civil service pensioners.

These people vote and they have a great deal of political clout. Chances of their cones going dry are virtually nil. If you had a business and your firm's customers were all DCF1s, you could safely plan five or ten years into the future. Luck would play a very small part in your sales, and your success would be almost totally dependent on your skills. DCF1s are the highest quality cones, and if there is any way for you to build them into your customer base, you should expend great efforts to do so. Their stability will make life much easier for you.

DCF2. A Deliberate Cone, Federally created and second (2nd) in line at the federal spigot. Examples are federal agencies or employees. These are very good cones because their incomes are straight from the federal spigot and backed by the printing press. However, these people occasionally experience the budget cuts, layoffs, and career changes that have little affect on DC1s, so they are not as stable or reliable as DC1s.

DCF3. A Deliberate Cone, Federally created and third (3rd) in line at the federal spigot. This is a firm or individual who earns his living selling directly to DCF1s and DCF2s. Examples would be military contractors, retailers located just outside the gates of military bases, and group insurance companies selling policies to federal employees. DCF3s can be valuable customers because their incomes do not fluctuate with the business cycle, but do not grow too dependent on them. They can be affected by federal budget cuts and layoffs.

DCL1. A Deliberate Cone, Locally (city or county) created and first (1st) in line at the local spigot. City and county pensioners. Not as good as state or federal, but some of the best.

DCL2. A Deliberate Cone, Local agencies or employees and second (2nd) in line at the state or local spigot.

DCL3. A firm or individual who earns his income by selling directly to DCL1s and DCL2s. Even further from the printing press, and so even less stable and reliable, but still resistant to the business cycle.

DCS1. A Deliberate Cone, State created and first (1st) in line at the state spigot. Examples would be state pensioners. Their incomes are stable and reliable, but because state governments cannot print money, they are not quite as reliable as DCF1s. Still, they are high quality, get them if you can.

DCS2. A Deliberate Cone, State created and second (2nd) in line at the state spigot. State agencies or employees.

DCS3. A Deliberate Cone, State created and third (3rd) in line at the state spigot. This is a firm or individual who earns his income by selling directly to DCS1s and DCS2s. These people can also be valuable customers because their incomes do not fluctuate with the business cycle, but they are further from the printing press than DCF3s and also vulnerable to budget cuts and layoffs. Much of the Sacramento economy in the 1980s was DCS3s.

DE-INDUSTRIALIZATION. The process of allowing the risks of owning plant and equipment to be shifted onto others. Instead of being called de-industrialization, it is often called restructuring, or sale-leaseback, outsourcing, vertical disaggregation, dynamic networking, or something else.

DELIBERATE CONE. Those created directly by government agencies injecting money into the economy in specific, *planned* locations.

DEMOGRAPHIC HOT SPOT. An identifiable group of individuals who have a lot of money to spend.

DEPRESSION. The correction period following an inflation. Usually includes a lot of business failures and unemployment.

D.E.W. LINE. Abbreviation for Distant Early Warning Line. From a line of radar stations constructed across Canada in the 1950s to watch for incoming Russian bombers.

DISCOUNT RATE. The discount rate is an interest rate and one of the Federal Reserve's tools for manipulating the money supply. A rising rate means a restricted money supply, and a falling rate means a rising money supply.

DISTANT EARLY WARNING LINE. A system of information sources capable of tracking the health and location of your cones. This way, anything that affects your cones will be detected before it can harm you. From a line of radar stations constructed across Canada in the 1950s to watch for incoming Russian bombers.

DOUBLE-CONE INVESTMENT. One that earns profits through two flows of money — capital gains and earnings. Examples of doubles are stocks, bonds, and commercial real estate. All earn money through their daily operations, and we also hope they rise in value, earning more money through capital gains.

EARNINGS. Income.

ECOLOGY. As it relates to the economy, the highly complex interrelationships among people.

ECONOMICS. The study of the production and distribution of wealth.

ECONOMY. The "economy" is seen by statists and other powerseekers as a kind of machine that can be adjusted or "fine tuned." In reality, the economy is a kind of ecology made of biological organisms — humans. Trying to fine tune or adjust them tends to damage them.

ENTREPRENEUR. The spark plug that makes the economy run. The person who searches for opportunities, takes risks, makes the important decisions and *organizes* land, labor, and capital. The essence of the firm.

ENTREPRENEURSHIP. The condition of being an entrepreneur, or the skills of an entrepreneur.

EQUITY. The portion of a property held free and clear by the owner.

EVIDENCE. Facts that tend to verify.

FACTORS OF PRODUCTION. Land, labor, capital, and entrepreneurship.

FASCISM. The belief that power holders should do whatever appears necessary, no exceptions, no limits. The political philosophy of the Roman Empire after about 31 BC.

FED. Abbreviation for Federal Reserve.

FEDERAL RESERVE. The central bank of the U.S.

FEDERAL RESERVE SYSTEM. The Federal Reserve system is the central bank of the U.S. Its primary purpose is to control short-term interest rates and the supply of money. It is called "the Fed" for short. "Tightening" means restricting the money supply, which drives up short-term interest rates. "Loosening" means expanding the money supply, which causes short-term rates to fall. This is because interest is the price of renting money. When the supply is tight the price rises. When it's loose, the price falls. The Fed controls tightness and looseness.

FILLED CONE. A cone that has lots of money running through it.

FIRST STAGE INFLATION. Also called stage one inflation. People save their money, waiting for prices to fall. Because they hold onto their money it doesn't enter the market to bid up prices. Little of the newly printed money is spent and prices cannot rise very fast.

FISCAL POLICY. The government's spending practices.

FIXED COSTS. "Overhead" — utilities, taxes, insurance, and other costs that cannot be easily reduced.

FORECAST. Prediction based on analysis of available data.

GEOGRAPHIC HOT SPOT. Areas — states, counties, cities, or neighborhoods — that receive large sums of money.

GNP. Gross National Product.

GROSS NATIONAL PRODUCT. The sum of all final goods and services produced in a nation. Does not include intermediate goods. Example: A car is a final good; the steel it contains is an intermediate good.

HOLLOW CONE. One with plant, equipment, and workers, but little money.

HOT SPOT. Demographic or geographic areas where new money is injected. These points of injection offer business, career, and investment opportunities.

HOUSE ORGAN. An internal company publication such as a newsletter for employees.

HYPERINFLATION. Runaway inflation.

I. Business Cycle Insensitive.

INFLATION. An increase in the amount of money. Causes the money to lose value, so prices rise.

INJECTION EFFECT. The change that occurs on Wall Street (the financial world) and Main Street (where most of us live and work) when the government injects new money into the economy.

INVISIBLE HAND. A term coined by Adam Smith to refer to the automatic way free markets organize production according to price signals.

JURIS NATURALISM. The belief that there is a natural law that determines the results of human conduct and this law is higher than any government's law.

KEYNESIAN ECONOMICS. Originally the economic philosophy of economist John Maynard Keynes. Today a kind of compromise, or middle road, between socialism and capitalism. Keynesians want broad government controls on economic activity, especially manipulation of the money supply. "Keynesian" is sometimes used as a synonym for "inflationist," or one who advocates inflating the money supply.

LABOR. Work. Also workers, in reference to unions.

LAND. In economics, includes not only terra firma but also the buildings, crops that might be growing on the land, minerals in it, or the fences around it. "Land" can also include rights to use sea lanes, or extract minerals from the sea or from under the sea, like oil.

LAW. Broadly speaking, the rules for human conduct that are enforced by violence or threats of violence. More narrowly, law sometimes means Common Law or Natural Law, as distinct from legislation. "A nation of laws and not of men" means a nation in which the highest law is Common Law or Natural Law, not legislation.

LEGISLATION. Made up law, as distinct from discovered law.

LEVERAGE. Money borrowed for a business venture or investment.

LIBERTY. Protection of the individual's right to his or her life, freedom, and property. Widespread obedience to the two fundamental laws that make civilization possible: (1) Do all you have agreed to do and (2) Do not encroach on other persons or their property.

LINE FUNCTIONS. Sales and production.

LOBBYIST. A person who hangs around the legislature lobby trying to secure the votes of lawmakers.

MALINVESTMENT. Investment that should not have happened.

MARGINALITY. The "straw that broke the camel's back" — tiny changes in taxes or regulations thousands of miles away can have severe, unforeseeable consequences on you or the people to whom you sell your goods or services.

MODEL. A mental picture of how the world works. Models are how we think, they are how we understand how the world works.

MONETARIST ECONOMICS. A free-market economic philosophy. Focuses on increases in money supply causing rising prices. Associated with the economics department of the University of Chicago; monetarism is sometimes called the Chicago school of economics.

MONETARY POLICY. The government's behavior in increasing or decreasing the supply of money.

MONEY. The most easily traded thing in a society. Economists call it the most liquid commodity. Money is the tool we use to measure and trade wealth.

MONEY DEMAND. The desire to own money.

MONEY SUPPLY. Amount of money in an economy.

NATURAL CONE. An area in which the supply of money is increasing due to normal increases in demand for a good or service, not due to injections of money by the government.

NET TAX PAYERS. People who pay more to the government than they get from the government.

NET TAX RECEIVERS. People who get more from the government than they pay to the government.

OUTSIDE SALES. Sales that occur in the field, at the customer's office, home, or job site.

OVERHEAD. Overhead is a rather nebulous term that generally refers to costs that are not directly attributable to the product and are not easily cut back. Opposite of variable cost. In automobile production, steel is a variable cost, and the fire insurance on the factory is overhead.

PAYBACK ANALYSIS. The procedure for determining the time required to recover the cost of a specific investment — the payback.

PER CAPITA. Per person.

POLITICAL LAW. Made up law. Same as legislation. Human law. Might makes right.

POLITICAL POWER. The privilege of using force on persons who have not harmed anyone. The legal privilege of backing one's decisions with violence or threats of violence, or the legal privilege of encroaching on the life, liberty, or property of a person who has not harmed anyone.

PONZI SCHEME. Named after swindler Charles Ponzi, a Ponzi scheme is one in which investors are paid not from income earned by the investment but from the contributions of new investors. Ponzis go broke when the number of new investors is no longer great enough to support the earlier investors. This is also called a pyramid scheme.

PRICE. An exchange rate.

PRODUCTION BOOM. Large expansion of production facilities.

PRODUCTION FUNCTION. Parts of a firm that create the goods or services.

QUALIFY. Making sure a possible customer is able to pay for the purchase.

REAL MONEY SUPPLY. Subtract price increases from money supply increases to get the "real" money supply.

RECESSION. The beginning of a depression that never went all the way.

REGULATORY POLICY. The government behavior in trying to control our work, our property and our investments.

RENT. Fee paid for the temporary use of something.

RUNAWAY INFLATION. A hyperinflation. Prices rising rapidly, every few days or hours.

S. Abbreviation for sinkhole.

SALES BOOM. Large expansion of sales.

SALES FUNCTION. The activity of trading a firm's goods or services for money.

SC. Abbreviation for a split cone.

SCIENTIFIC LAW. Verbal or mathematical expressions of Natural Law learned through observation, study, and experimentation.

SECOND STAGE INFLATION. Also called stage two inflation. Money changes hands faster. A little bit of money is beginning to do the work of a lot of money. Prices start rising faster than the money is printed.

S.I.C. CODES. Abbreviation for Standard Industrial Classification codes.

SHARES OF STOCK. Certificates of ownership in a corporation.

SINKHOLE. A depressed area. An area from which more wealth is removed than is poured back in.

SINGLE CONE INVESTMENTS. Investments are those that earn profits only through capital gains. Examples are commodities, undeveloped land, currencies, art, and antiques.

SOMEWHAT BUSINESS CYCLE SENSITIVE. Income affected by the boom-and-bust cycle, but not seriously.

SPECIALIZATION OF LABOR. Each individual spending most of his work time on a single job.

SPLIT CONE. A cone that falls between Deliberate and Accidental Cones.

STAFF FUNCTIONS. Support for the line function includes accounting, finance, legal, personnel, administration, etc.

STANDARD INDUSTRIAL CLASSIFICATION CODES. For data processing purposes, the Federal Government classifies each industry and occupation according to S.I.C. codes (Standard Industrial Classification codes).

STANDARDS OF PROOF. Measures of authenticity.

STATISM. The opposite of the original American philosophy. Statism says political power is a good thing and everyone should have some. Government is our friend, our protector, the solution to our problems. Force is the tool for enforcement. There is no law higher than the government's law.

STATIST. One who believes in government as the solution to problems. Statists assume the benefits of government activities can be greater than total costs.

STORE. A building in which goods are kept safe until they are sold from the building.

STREAMLINE. To shape for fast and easy movement.

SUBSIDY. Money given to a person or organization who did not earn it.

SUPER CLIPPER STRATEGY. Buying from sinkholes and selling to cones.

SW. Somewhat business cycle sensitive.

TAX. The way governments get money. To tax means to take money away from someone, by force if necessary, even if he thinks what he is getting in return has little or no value.

THEORY. Coherent set of ideas that seem to explain a reality.

THIRD STAGE INFLATION. Also called stage three inflation. Money changes hands very fast. People don't want it and they are trying to get rid of it. Money demand is falling like a stone and velocity is skyrocketing. No one can stop the money from losing its value. Even if the printing presses are stopped, the money becomes worthless because no one wants it. It ends when people completely reject the money and begin using something new for money.

V. Very business cycle sensitive.

VARIABLE COSTS. Variable costs are those that increase incrementally as units are produced. These can include raw materials, electricity, production wages, transportation, and others. These are added to the fixed costs to determine the firm's total costs.

VELOCITY. The speed at which money changes hands.

VERY BUSINESS CYCLE SENSITIVE. Income seriously affected by the boom-and-bust cycle.

WEALTH. Goods and services — food, clothing, haircuts, cars, TVs, homes, and everything else that makes life better. Not to be confused with money. Money can be wealth, but it is only one kind.

ZERO SUM GAME. An activity in which one person can win only if another person loses.

About Richard J. Maybury

Richard Maybury, also known as Uncle Eric, is a world renowned author, lecturer and geopolitical analyst. He consults with business firms in the U.S. and Europe. Richard is the former Global Affairs editor of MONEYWORLD and widely regarded as one of the finest free-market writers in America. Mr. Maybury's articles have appeared in THE WALL STREET JOURNAL, USA TODAY, and other major publications.

Richard Maybury has penned eleven books in the Uncle Eric series. His books have been endorsed by top business leaders including former U.S. Treasury Secretary William Simon, and he has been interviewed on more than 250 radio and TV shows across America.

He has been married for more than 35 years, has lived abroad, traveled around the world, and visited 48 states and 40 countries.

He is truly a teacher for all ages.

Index

Index **269**

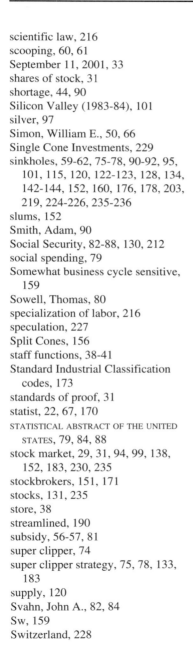

"...the entire [Uncle Eric] series should be a required, integral, component of the social studies curriculum in all public and private schools. This would bring a quantum leap upward in the quality of citizenship in this country in a single generation."

—William P. Snavely
Emeritus Professor of Economics
George Mason University

Study Guides and / or Tests available (or forthcoming)

for the Uncle Eric books

Each study guide will include some, and at times all, of the following:

1) Chapter-by-chapter comprehension questions

2) Research activities

3) A list of films

4) Thought questions

5) Final exam

Order from your favorite book store or direct from the publisher:

Bluestocking Press
www.BluestockingPress.com

(See contact information on the last page of this book.)

"Uncle Eric is on my top 10 list of homeschool resources."
— William Cormier
Freelance Writer for homeschool publications

"None of my kids are graduating from high school until they've finished reading all these books. Very highly recommended." (5 hearts)
— Mary Pride, PRACTICAL HOMESCHOOLING MAGAZINE

Bluestocking Press

Bluestocking Press publishes the following:

1) Richard J. Maybury's Uncle Eric books (and the accompanying student study guides for the Uncle Eric books)

2) Karl Hess' CAPITALISM FOR KIDS

3) Kathryn Daniels' COMMON SENSE BUSINESS FOR KIDS

4) ECONOMICS: A FREE MARKET READER

5) LAURA INGALLS WILDER AND ROSE WILDER LANE HISTORICAL TIMETABLE

Visit the BLUESTOCKING PRESS CATALOG online at
www.BluestockingPress.com

To order by phone, contact Bluestocking Press
(See contact information
on the last page of this book.)

Published by Bluestocking Press

Uncle Eric Books by Richard J. Maybury

UNCLE ERIC TALKS ABOUT PERSONAL, CAREER, AND FINANCIAL SECURITY
WHATEVER HAPPENED TO PENNY CANDY?
WHATEVER HAPPENED TO JUSTICE?
ARE YOU LIBERAL? CONSERVATIVE? OR CONFUSED?
ANCIENT ROME: HOW IT AFFECTS YOU TODAY
EVALUATING BOOKS: WHAT WOULD THOMAS JEFFERSON THINK ABOUT THIS?
THE MONEY MYSTERY
THE CLIPPER SHIP STRATEGY
THE THOUSAND YEAR WAR IN THE MIDEAST
WORLD WAR I: THE REST OF THE STORY
WORLD WAR II: THE REST OF THE STORY

Bluestocking Guides (study guides for the Uncle Eric books)
by Jane A. Williams and/or Kathryn Daniels
Each Study Guide includes some or all of the following:
1) chapter-by-chapter comprehension questions and answers
2) application questions and answers
3) research activities
4) essay assignments
5) thought questions
6) final exam

More Bluestocking Press Titles

LAURA INGALLS WILDER AND ROSE WILDER LANE HISTORICAL TIMETABLE
CAPITALISM FOR KIDS: GROWING UP TO BE YOUR OWN BOSS by Karl Hess
COMMON SENSE BUSINESS FOR KIDS by Kathryn Daniels
ECONOMICS: A FREE MARKET READER edited by Jane Williams & Kathryn Daniels

Order information: Order any of the above by phone or online from:

Bluestocking Press
Phone: 800-959-8586
email: CustomerService@BluestockingPress.com
web site: www.BluestockingPress.com